Helping Hands, Helping Hearts

*Opportunity Village is like phyllo dough; there are a million layers to it.
Everyone who has ever walked this place has his own story, and each story
is unique and different. Each one forms a separate layer.*

— Cary J. Harned
Grants & Major Gifts Officer

Stephens Press • Las Vegas, Nevada

Helping Hands Helping Hearts

The Story of Opportunity Village

Jack Harpster

Designer: Sue Campbell
Publishing Coordinator: Stacey Fott
Cover Photographer: Richard Bailey
Cover Model: Georgina Hulme

ISBN 10: 1-932173-63-3
ISBN 13: 978-1-9321736-35

Cataloging in Publication.

Harpster, Jack.
Helping hands, helping hearts : the story of Opportunity Village / Jack Harpster.
184 p. : ill., photos ; 24 cm.
Includes bibliographic references.
Contents: The founder – The history – The beginning – The early struggles – Opportunity
Village – Staff & volunteers – Vocational training – Employment – The clients – The commu-
nity – The big event – The economics – The future.
Summary: Provides the history and programs for the mentally and physically disabled pro-
vided by Opportunity Village, founded by the efforts of Al and Dessie Bailey.

ISBN: 1-932173-63-3
ISBN-10: 978-1-932173-63-5

1. Opportunity Village (Las Vegas, Nev.) 2. People with disabilities—Services for—Nevada.
3. People with mental disabilities—Services for—Nevada. 4. Bailey, Elbert.

362.4 dc22   2007   2006931008

STEPHENS PRESS, LLC
A Stephens Media Company

Post Office Box 1600
Las Vegas, NV 89125-1600
www.stephenspress.com

Printed in Hong Kong

DEDICATION

This book is dedicated to people with intellectual disabilities who radiate hope and aspiration. They are the reason Opportunity Village began in 1954 and the reason it will continue for decades to come. They have made this a better, kinder and more accepting world.

"Opportunity waits behind this door; all you have to do is knock"

Opportunity Village holds a special place in the heart of every Nevadan. It certainly holds a special place in mine. The brave parents who first came forward in 1954 and said that their children with intellectual disabilities deserved to live good, fulfilling lives, founded a tiny organization serving thousands of people with disabilities in award-winning programs that teach job skills, employ them in good jobs and offer needed services. The organization saves Nevada and its citizens millions of dollars every year by doing this privately. Opportunity Village has rewarded Nevada by making it a better place for every citizen, regardless of his or her level of ability.

— U.S. Senator Harry Reid of Nevada

Contents

Acknowledgments

I'd like to thank all the people who gave unstintingly of their time to sit for interviews and photographs for this book.

First and foremost, this includes the clients of Opportunity Village, a group of men and women who I now realize are little different from all the other men and women who have come into and out of my life over the past seventy years. I thoroughly enjoyed every minute I spent with each one of them; and I thank them for their patience and understanding as I strove to better understand their lives.

I'd also like to thank the fine staff of employees and volunteers at Opportunity Village, and all those benevolent community members who so ardently support the work of this extraordinary organization. I especially thank those older members of the community whose recollections of the earliest days of the organization are so crisp and clear after more than fifty years. Without fail, each one of them that I interviewed apologized beforehand about how little they recalled; but as soon as the conversations began, all the memories came flooding back. Their memories were full of priceless anecdotes that added character to the story.

I'd also like to offer special thanks to two organizations that were particularly helpful to me. First, Brian Janis and his crew of talented associates at Phototechnik International took many of the photographs you'll see throughout the book — pro bono, of course — as they have done for Opportunity Village for more than two decades. And finally, Jason Smith, executive director of Variety, the Children's Charity, graciously lent me a tremendous amount of historical material from the group's outstanding early scrapbook collection.

—JH

FOREWORD

Opportunity Village has been named "Best Community Organization" for ten years running by *Review-Journal* readers in our annual Best of Las Vegas awards. There is a reason.

Opportunity Village's hands-on, hearts-open outlook permeates our community. Its leaders are tireless advocates for individuals with disabilities. The difference that Opportunity Village makes in the life of a person with severe disabilities is priceless. The organization gives individuals work experience, marketable job skills, independence, and the pride of accomplishment.

Thanks to the support of world-renowned entertainers, Las Vegas businesses and ordinary folks, families of people with disabilities proudly see their loved ones gain self esteem and achieve things once not thought possible.

The *Las Vegas Review-Journal* is honored to support the publication of *Helping Hands, Helping Hearts.*

— Sherman Frederick, Publisher
Las Vegas Review-Journal

INTRODUCTION

The sudden sound was ear piercing, and in combination with the brightly flashing strobe lights, I found it momentarily unnerving. My tour guide and I had been heading into the Project PRIDE room, where the most profoundly disabled clients were tended, when the fire alert system suddenly went off. I immediately asked if it was a drill, and Cary Harned, my guide, assured me it was not. It was a real fire warning.

My first thought was of the hundreds of adults with intellectual disabilities at work, play or rest in the large facility. My tour had already taken us through the immaculate food service training area, where a number of clients were learning new culinary skills. And we had gone through the large, seemingly chaotic packaging and assembly warehouse. Here, sixty or more men and women were diligently labeling, folding and packaging emerald green print pajamas as part of a current work contract. How could they possibly get out in a quick and orderly fashion between the long lines of work space tables, I wondered.

I was a complete novice at this time. It was my first tour of Opportunity Village, and I admit I badly miscalculated the level of competency of these men and women who were intellectually disabled, and their dedicated staff. Cary and I opened a large set of double doors leading to the warehouse — no more than fifteen seconds had elapsed since the alarm was tripped — and already a stream of orderly, well-organized people was heading our way. There was little talking, and absolutely none of the horseplay I recalled occurring during my school fire drills years earlier. Those with physical disabilities, struggling with walkers, canes or wheelchairs, were being lovingly helped along by other clients, their friends and work mates. Many held their hands over their ears; Cary told me the screeching sound and the flashing lights frighten most of the clients; but you could not tell it from their calm demeanors.

We were now in the lobby, and from every side doors opened and similar groups moved quickly toward the exits. From the Project PRIDE room, attendants were lifting and carrying the profoundly disabled from their room. Cary and I hurried outside with the others, and I found a spot on a bench while she went about her emergency duties. A passing attendant told me their goal from start to finish was three minutes once the alarm sounded; and they had easily bested the mark on this crisp December morning. The clients assembled comfortably into two large knots at each end of the facility, exactly where they had been trained to go. There was a little grinning and chuckling, and some nervous laughter, but complete order. The precision of the drill, and absolute discipline by each individual, was a source of pride with them, you could tell.

When the alarm was finally quieted — burning popcorn had been the innocuous culprit — a small cheer went up, and the clients clapped happily. So did I.

This small vignette transpired just as I was beginning to write this book, but it came at an ideal time and provided a very valuable insight for me. I did not see helpless, long-suffering souls being herded out of a burning building. I saw capable, well-trained, disciplined men and women react to a normal emergency task with a level of intelligence and loving care that would put most "normal" members of our society to shame.

It was a lesson I would carry with me throughout the remainder of this rewarding project.

Opportunity Village invites both residents and non-residents to tour their campuses and see first-hand how one of the most unique not-for-profit organizations in the nation operates. It is a very worthwhile thing to do.

Union Pacific Railroad apprentices and their instructors in the late 1920s.

CHAPTER ONE

The Founder:
Why Our Daughter?

Claud and Bertha Bailey's initial impression of Las Vegas as they first stepped off the train from East Los Angeles was anything but positive.

It was the early 1920s. Claud had accepted a job as an engineer with the Union Pacific, a good job that brought him and his family to the Mojave Desert community, then only a dusty whistle stop in the middle of nowhere. Bertha hadn't expected a paradise; but she was still surprised at the scattered settlement of wood frame houses, concrete block cottages, tent houses and small scrub trees spread across the harsh landscape. Their small son Elbert was only six; and to him the idea of living in a remote desert outpost was very exciting, while his older sister Gertude was already missing her friends back home, as is the way of preteen girls.

Las Vegas itself was only about fifteen years old when the Baileys arrived, instantly qualifying the family as pioneers in the small town. It had been founded in 1905 when the San Pedro, Los Angeles & Salt Lake Railroad (SPLA&SL) first auctioned off lots so a town could be built around the depot where their trains could pause for servicing and the train crews housed. The SPLA&SL was jointly owned by the Union Pacific and William A. Clark and his younger brother. The elder Clark had made his first fortune in copper mining on his fabulous Anaconda claim in Montana.

Just before the Baileys arrived, the Clarks had sold their share of the railroad to the Union Pacific (UP), which was now the sole owner of the promising route from Los Angeles to Salt Lake City. By this time, the population of the town had swelled to 4,900 people, and although it had grown since its founding, it was still basically a railroad town.

Among the attractive UP benefits that had brought Claud and Bertha to the desert was the promise of low cost housing. The railroad had built a string of single story, concrete block-and-plank cottages that were rented or sold exclusively to railroad employees, and the Baileys moved into one of them. The well maintained cottage district was the nicest neighborhood in town, and every small home had two or three cottonwood trees to insure shade. The Baileys probably rented their first home — according to Joan Whitely in *Young Las Vegas* they would have paid about $20 a month.

Another attractive benefit the UP promised was free train service for the entire family back to Southern California, so the Baileys would be able maintain some of their close friendships with the folks back home. Claud was an engineer, first on steam driven engines, then later on diesel locomotives; and he was assigned the Las Vegas to Los Angeles run.

The couple had scarcely gotten settled before they decided to move to another house at 311½ North 7th Street, a tiny one bedroom. There they rented from a rather unusual desert couple, Sam and Katie Griffin. Sam was British, and Katie from Palestine, and the two couples became good friends.

It was a good life, and Las Vegas was becoming a nice place to live. According to a 1926 article in the *Las Vegas Review*, the town had five churches, two banks, two newspapers, electric lighting and telephone service, a fine public library and "all the improvements of a modern community."

Elbert, now called "Al," grew up and attended school with the children of other pioneer families: the Von Tobels, the Brackens, the Cashmans, the Squires, and the Martins, among others. It was a good life, despite the harsh summer conditions, and the Baileys would remain even after Claud had retired from the Union Pacific.

In 1936 another newcomer arrived in Las Vegas. Dessie Bassette was the seventh of eight children of Henry and Sarah Bassette who owned a prairie farm in Burlington, Kit Carson County, Colorado.

We are indebted to a speech made in Dessie's honor in 1963 by pioneer female journalist Florence Lee Jones for the little we know about Dessie's early life in Colorado. Farm life was difficult. From the age of six, Dessie herded cattle on horseback every day, winter and summer, to help the farm sustain her large family. When she was only eleven, the country was suddenly sucked into the Great Depression. Tales of ruined businessmen jumping from tall buildings, and families devastated by spiraling stock prices, are commonplace. But family farms were not immune from the economic disaster that followed. Farm prices fell by more than fifty percent during the early years of the Depression; and just as farmers were beginning to see some light at the end of the tunnel, a severe drought hit the nation's Great Plains, followed by savage dust and wind storms that ravaged the area, which became known as the "Dust Bowl." Henry Bassette's farm was caught in the middle of these twin hells, sitting as it did in east central Colorado just miles from the Kansas border.

Dessie graduated from the eighth grade when she was thirteen. The valedictorian of her class, she was an excellent student and took pride in her studies. But as most of her classmates headed to high school, Dessie's formal education would be over. She had to find work to help support the family. There were no regular jobs available in Burlington, so Dessie went from farm to farm hiring herself out for whatever tasks were offered. She milked cows, baked bread, did housework and gardening, and performed other hard chores that were assigned to her. Dessie earned from $2.50 to $3.00 a week for her labors, a paltry sum but an amount that helped keep the Bassette's sinking fortunes from going completely under.

In the mid 1930s Dessie's older sister Mary moved to Las Vegas. For Henry and Sarah Bassette, it was a sad time seeing their family splinter, but it would be one less mouth to feed. Mary's regular letters home were full of the excitement of life in the "big city," so in 1937 Dessie decided to visit her. She had just turned eighteen.

Las Vegas was a revelation. A new law had just been passed setting a minimum daily wage of $3.00 for women. It didn't take the valedictorian long to figure out that she could make as much in one day in Las

Vegas as she made all week on the Colorado farm; and she decided to stay for good.

The city Dessie decided to call home had launched its future as one of America's truly unique cities in 1931, a banner year for the small town in the Mojave Desert. That year, Las Vegas had legalized gambling, and construction had begun on the Boulder (Hoover) Dam, fifteen miles southeast of town. In 1935, President Roosevelt had joined other dignitaries and the dam — one of the engineering marvels of modern history — was officially dedicated.

The late 1930s were an exciting time, and Las Vegas was an exciting town for a young farm girl. The city had grown to around 8,000 residents, and jobs

One of the Las Vegas Elks very first Helldorado parades in the mid 1930s passes by the Vegas Sweet Shoppe where Opportunity Village founder Dessie Bailey found her first job. Photograph courtesy of Davis Collection, University of Nevada, Las Vegas Library.

were plentiful. Dessie found a job at the Vegas Sweet Shoppe at 111 Fremont Street, right next door to the White Spot Cafe, and settled into her new life.

Historians Eugene Moehring and Michael Green described the city at that time in their *Las Vegas: A Centennial History:*

> In the 1930s and early 1940s, a spate of residential construction helped the city shed its old railroad-town image. Housing became more diverse, and the architectural style reflected the prosperity the dam and war economies created. The area south of Fremont housed some of the city's most prominent lawyers, political leaders, and businessmen. It also contained larger buildings such as Dr. Roy Martin's mission-revival Las Vegas Hospital . . . the new Las Vegas High . . . [and] the Huntridge Theater.

> While population concentrated around downtown for many years, other neighbor-hoods developed farther out . . . the old Boulder, Southern, and Meadows Additions began attract-ing residents during and after World War I, and many more in the 1920s and 1930s.

Las Vegas, like most cities and towns around the country, had also taken advantage of the money available under President Roosevelt's New Deal to make much-needed civic improvements. Streets were paved, sewers expanded into the burgeoning suburbs, and parks and public buildings erected.

A highlight of 1935 was the first Elks Helldorado parade and rodeo (actually, the rodeo would be added during the second year,) a community-wide celebra-tion of the city's western heritage that was intended to attract more tourists to the new gambling mecca. It was so successful that the event would be held annu-ally for the next sixty-four years.

The same year Dessie arrived in town, Al Bailey was attending Las Vegas High School. Following high school, he found a job as a fry cook at the Town Barbeque; and as luck would have it, his path crossed with the young farm girl from Colorado. Dessie was a vivacious brunette, smart as a whip, and a hard and persistent worker at anything she tackled. She was taken with the muscular young man who was bronzed by the glaring south-western sun, and a proper courtship followed. In July 1938 the two were wed.

Al now had additional responsibilities, so in 1939 he found a better position with the Nevada State Highway Division. He had also signed on with the Las Vegas Volunteer Fire Department, a position he took very seriously, and he would serve for seventeen years in that capacity.

There was only one problem with Al's new job: they assigned him to a post building roads near Lathrop Wells, only a dot on the Nevada map nearly one hundred tortuous, dusty miles northwest of Las Vegas. The young couple decided to try and make it work, seeing each other whenever possible. But it was a strain, particularly for newlyweds. All that changed however, as World War II approached.

In 1941 Al tried to enlist in the Army, but failed the physical exam. He would have to sit on the side-lines throughout the war, a bitter pill for the consci-entious young man. Rather than return to Lathrop Wells, he sought and gained a position where his

Dessie was a vivacious brunette, smart as a whip, and a hard and persistent worker at anything she tackled.

Al and Dessie Bailey's first home in Las Vegas, at 711 Sixth Street.

dad had worked for many years, the Union Pacific Railroad, as a messenger. It wasn't much of a job, but at least it was home, and close to his new wife. Al loved the freight trains best; and over the years he would be promoted to brakeman, then to conductor. He remained with the UP until his retirement in 1976.

Now that he was home, Al and Dessie decided to buy a house. They had managed to save enough for a modest down payment, so with some trepidation the young couple bought an unpretentious frame house with a stucco exterior at 711 South Sixth Street. The house cost $7,000. Son Pat Bailey remembers the home being desert rose in color.

The war years were an unexpected boon to the small desert town. The opening of Basic Magnesium (BMI) in nearby Henderson, added nearly fifteen thousand people to the local population, according to historians Moehring and Green; and the establishment of the Las Vegas Army Air Corps Gunnery School northeast of town formed the backbone of what would eventually become Nellis Air Force Base. Las Vegas was now, and for all time, more than just a railroad town.

In 1944 Al and Dessie had their first child, a son they named Patrick Henry. He was a handsome little fellow, and very bright. Even as a small child, he loved books, and he was already reading and spelling at the fifth grade level by kindergarten.

Pat recalled an incident when he was still a tot, perhaps during the winter of 1946–1947. Uncharacteristically, it had snowed long and hard the night before, and Pat remembered standing on the couch looking out the large picture window. Dessie had awakened early — Al was already at work — and she was outside building a snowman.

"She took one of my cowboy hats, plus some tinker toys for eyes, mouth, etc.," he recalled; "then she came back in and dressed me in every scrap of clothing I had, and took me outside with the camera."

Dessie plopped Pat beside the snowman and stepped back to take a black-and-white snapshot of the very untypical desert scene. Even today, some sixty years later, Pat still remembers the scene with a chuckle: the sky was light and cloudless, the photo's background snow white, and there was no sunlight to cast shadows. What appeared in the snapshot, once it was developed, was a well-bundled kid standing beside some tinker toys and a cowboy hat that seemed to be suspended in the air. "On closer examination," Pat explained, "you can make out the snowman — but at first glimpse, it's Penn and Teller time!"

These would be the happiest, most unfettered times in the life of the young family. Only a short time later, Dessie's mother Sarah passed away at the farm in Colorado. Perhaps her father Henry had simply had enough of farming life; he had managed to survive the Great Depression, the drought and the dust storms that had plagued his Kit Carson County farmlands. Or perhaps with Sarah's passing, there were just too many memories there for him. In either case, he sold the farm and moved to Las Vegas to be close to his two daughters. Mary had taken a husband by this time; and she and W. H. "Rudy" Rudolph fixed up a spare room in their home, and Henry moved in. The

After only a few months, Dessie could tell that Claudia was "different."

Rudolphs owned and operated the first hunting and fishing shop in town, called the Outdoor Equipment Company, at 1625 Fremont Street. Henry helped around the store, and spent a lot of time with his new grandson, Pat.

It was good having so much family surrounding them, and Dessie and Al Bailey looked forward to the future. But in 1947, that happy future crashed down around them. Their second child, a daughter they named Claudia, was born. After only a few months, Dessie could tell that Claudia was "different." She was slow to respond, often lethargic, and her almond-shaped eyes didn't seem to focus well.

"Elbert thought her hands were different and her eyes had a slant to them," Dessie told a *Las Vegas Review-Journal* reporter in a 1983 article about her pioneering activities for people with intellectual disabilities.

"I had to force-feed her until she was three months old. Finally she got the idea and would bawl when she was hungry," Dessie continued.

The doctors in Las Vegas, even her own family doctor, were no help. "The doctor here told his nurses he felt so bad about Claudia that he couldn't tell us the truth," she recalled. "We didn't know exactly what was wrong with her, but we knew something wasn't right." So the Baileys took Claudia to a specialist in Long Beach, California.

"The specialist gave it to us straight," she said. "He said she was born with an intellectual disability. It was as though a black curtain suddenly dropped down in front of me that shut out all light, all hope and I wondered if I would ever sleep again, or if I could go on living." But then the doctor told them something they would never forget: 'Don't feel sorry for those kids. Feel sorry for the kids who have the mentality but don't use it."

Claudia was a Down syndrome child. As the Baileys would later learn, she was one of the approximately three percent of American children born with an intellectual disability.

In order to get even the vaguest idea of what Al and Dessie would have been going through in those early years, we can look to Sarason and Doris's writings about the parents of the retarded infant:

> Preoccupied with their own altered needs, plagued with anxiety, guilt, and anger, searching the past for reasons and the present for hope, they cannot evade the knowledge that planning and hoping are frail needs on which to restructure lives. Experiencing those too frequent, piercing reminders that by virtue of someone coming into their lives a good deal has gone out of it and they must bury treasured hopes and fantasies — caught up in a swirl of personal despair, it is the rare parent who can respond unanxiously, spontaneously, and competently to the infant. When you are absorbed with yourself and your future, a limit is set to what you can be aware of and respond to in others. To give of yourself to someone else when you feel you need so much of it for yourself is extraordinarily difficult, if not impossible.

Without a doubt, Al and Dessie Bailey felt all those swirling needs and emotions.

But they clung tenaciously to the encouraging words they had heard from their California doctor, words that launched Dessie Bailey on a lifelong quest to help her daughter, and others like her, make the very best of what God had given them.

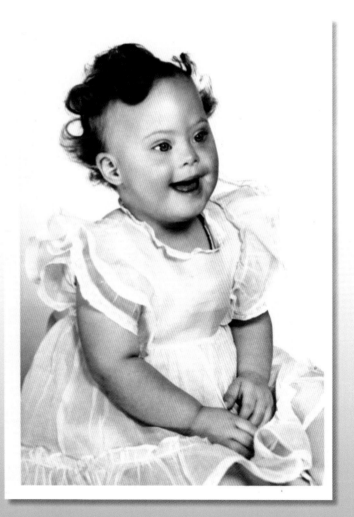

Claudia Bailey, the baby that started it all.

Artwork by Tiffany,
project ENABLE client,
Walters Family Campus.

CHAPTER TWO

The History:
Mental Retardation, the Hidden Disability

Mental retardation is not something you have, like blue eyes, or a bad heart.
Nor is it something you are, like short, or thin.
It is not a medical disorder, nor a mental disorder.
Mental retardation is a particular state of functioning that begins in childhood
and is characterized by limitation in both intelligence and adaptive skills.
Mental retardation reflects the "fit" between the capabilities of individuals and
the structure and expectations of their environment.
— American Association on Mental Retardation (AAMR)

The AAMR's official definition of mental retardation states, "Mental retardation is a disability characterized by significant limitations both in intellectual functioning and in adaptive behavior as expressed in conceptual, social, and practical adaptive skills. This disability originates before age eighteen."

The AAMR's website (www.AAMR.org) declares they have altered their definition of mental retardation ten times since 1908, based upon new information, clinical breakthroughs or scientific research findings.

Intellectual disability is characterized by significantly sub-average intellectual functioning, which exists concurrently with related limitations in two or more of the following adaptive skills: communication, self-care, home living, social skills, community use, self-direction, health and safety, functional academics, leisure, and work.

People with intellectual disabilities are generally classified into four subgroups, depending upon their Intelligence Quotient, or IQ. A person with an IQ of 70 or less is considered intellectually disabled. The subgroups, and the percentage of the people who fall into each subgroup on the national level, are:

Mild: IQ 55-69 (85 percent)
Moderate: IQ 40-54 (10 percent)
Severe: IQ 25-39 (5 percent)
Profound: IQ 0-24 (<1 percent)

The AAMR's most recent findings estimate a general incidence of mental retardation births at 125,000 per year, which corresponds to approximately three percent of the population. They are quick to admit however that the research is scant. A recent comprehensive Canadian study of their maritime provinces found a prevalence of 3.65 per thousand. Because most children with intellectual disabilities are considered "mild," at the high end of the IQ range (85%,) it's probable the figure is even higher, with many children who are considered by their parents as simply "slow" in reality falling at or below 69 IQ.

In Clark County, the figure is thought to be three percent, right at the national average.

Intellectual disabilities are the most widespread disabilities in the world; it is thirty-five times more common than muscular dystrophy and twelve times more common than a physical disability.

By definition, intellectual disability occurs during a child's developmental period. However, older children, or even adults, may become disabled after a traumatic brain injury or illness. Older adults who lose their mental faculties are more likely diagnosed with age-related disabilities.

The causes of mental retardation are many, and complex. The base causes include chromosomal abnormalities, genetic defects, intrauterine, perinatal, neonatal and postnatal causes. It is not within the scope of this book to delve into that area, nor will we list all the disorders that comprise mental retardation. However, the most prevalent disorders are caused by chromosomal abnormalities, and of those, Down syndrome is the most frequently occurring.

The most recent study of birth defects, published in 2006 by the Center for Disease Control and Prevention, states that Down syndrome occurs in one of every 733 live births in the United States. It had been previously believed that the figure was one in every 800 to 1,000 live births. The risk for Down syndrome increases with the age of the mother, from an estimated 1 in 2,000 among twenty-year olds to 1 in 100 for forty-year olds. The statistics were gathered from a representative sample of eleven states for the years 1999, 2000 and 2001.

The most frequently occurring conditions observed in the clients of Opportunity Village in Las Vegas are Down syndrome, cerebral palsy, autism, and fetal alcohol syndrome.

It is very important that people who are not familiar with mental retardation understand an important distinction. Mental retardation ***is not*** the same as mental illness. It is true that many people with intellectual disabilities also have a mental illness; but the two things are completely different and separate. We have already described mental retardation. Association of Retarded Citizens (ARC), one of the nation's top organizations for children and adults with intellectual and developmental disabilities, define mental illnesses as "severe disturbances of behavior, mood, thought processes and/or social and interpersonal relationships."

It is also estimated that people with intellectual disabilities have a forty percent chance of also having a physical disability, such as congenital heart defect, respiratory illness, and hearing, speech and/or sight impairment.

Sarason and Doris said, "Precisely because mental retardation is a socially invented concept, the people who have 'it' have to be seen in relation to those who do not have 'it.'" They continued, "... if we want to understand the concept of mental retardation and those who are called mentally retarded, we have to understand ourselves and our society in historical terms."

The history of the treatment of people with intellecual disabilities in this country is not a proud one. It has plagued man for as long as he has walked upright. We can find stories of "simpletons" or "idiots" as far back in literature as one may delve. Some are written with humor, and despite the political incorrectness of it, they bring a smile to your face; others are written with pathos, and they bring a tear to your eye. Perhaps the first writing in America on the subject of mental retardation was a 1681 Boston printing of English preacher John Bunyan's story, *The Pilgrim's Progress*, penned while its author languished in prison for preaching the gospel without permission.

Bunyan wrote of the allegorical journey of his characters, a mixed group of men and women who represented *everyman* and *everywoman*. One of his characters was Mr. Feeblemind, whom, in the company of the other pilgrims, was treated as an equal, not a deviant.

Such was the worldview of those victims of mental retardation in earliest colonial America. The village idiot, or simpleton, may have been taunted by the children of the village, but he was protected and cared for by his family. If he had no family, he was cared for by other families of the village. It was a case of simple Christian benevolence. As long as American life was rurally centered in small towns and farms, people with intellectual disabilities were not feared, shunned or particularly singled out in any specific way.

The village idiot, or simpleton, may have been taunted by the children of the village, but he was protected and cared for by his family.

In the second quarter of the nineteenth century, that began to change. Towns had become cities all along the eastern seaboard, and the Midwest and South were beginning to follow suit. Where once all Americans had been completely self-sufficient, or had survived within a barter system, now commerce and currency were king.

The feebleminded, as they were by then called, were becoming a social problem, and a costly one.

James Trent, in his fine study *Inventing the Feeble Mind: A History of Mental Retardation in the United States,* tells how, by this period, the country had come to identify all of it dependent people as being in one of two groups. There were the "worthy" dependents — orphans, widows and those with intellectual disabilities — and "unworthy" dependents — the unemployed and the criminals. Only their "worthiness" distinguished one group from the other, and only the worthy group received local assistance. This charitable aid most often came in the form of a publicly funded almshouse, where the worthy dependents could be warehoused.

All this began to change with the Financial Panic of 1837, the longest and deepest economic recession the country would see up until the Great Depression. With unemployment high, the poor — previously viewed as unworthy — moved up a notch and began finding themselves in the almshouses in ever-growing numbers. To compensate, new institutions began to spring up to serve individual groups that were being forced out of the almshouse system: orphan asylums, state operated schools for the blind, deaf and dumb, and penitentiaries.

It was in France where the first attempts were made to educate and improve the conditions. St. Vincent De Paul was perhaps the first man to try, in the priory of St. Lazarus, in the seventeenth century. In the early nineteenth century, in Bicetre, France, the first successful "school for idiots" began to serve them by educating and training them, a whole new concept for the time. It had been previously assumed that idiocy could not be treated, that idiots could not learn, simply because they had no minds.

Edouard Seguin was the man whose vision launched that first successful experiment. He had been a student of the pioneering French doctor Jean Itard, an early pioneer in working with mental retardation, and whose story of working with "the wild boy of Aveyron" would gain him worldwide attention. Seguin would move to America in 1850, after a number of schools had opened here. His approach to teaching the people with intellectual disabilities, a method he described as physiological, used the body's own physical resources to bring about a change in behavior. This "education of the senses" and "education of motion" would be adapted by Italian doctor Maria Montessori in the development of her now-widespread teaching methods used for all children ever since.

By the first quarter of the twentieth century, however, all of these promising beginnings had evaporated. For a host of social, political, and economic reasons, care of the mentally retarded had lapsed into a function of custodial care only. Education and training had fallen by the wayside despite their early promise, as we can see in a 1909 letter from Charles T. Wilbur, superintendent of a home in Illinois, to a colleague:

> The ideas concerning the aims and objects for the institutions for the Feeble-minded are very different from what they formerly were. The whole aim of society is now to drive them into Colonies with very little effort as to their mental development.
>
> Now when thus congregated in Droves like cattle it is about as much as we can accomplish to keep them comfortable and fed and clothed after a fashion . . . God help the Defectives of the land as man is failing to make much effort.

Most public institutions, designed to care for hundreds of "inmates" at a time, were by now caring for populations in the thousands. The range of ages had also grown considerably, as had the range of disability of the inmates. The early schools had sought to train only those with mild disabilities; now the populations went from those who were just considered "slow" to those with profound disabilities in the lowest IQ ranges.

. . . God help the Defectives of the land as man is failing to make much effort.

The fabric of society was undergoing radical changes as well. Two social phenomena — one very promising and one quite frightening — had their roots at the dawning of the twentieth century.

The scary one, rooted in social Darwinism, spurred the first interest in eugenics. The term refers to a movement or social policy advocating the improvement of human hereditary traits through society's intervention. This can run the scale from the rather benign fact of voluntary birth control to such Draconian measures as genetic engineering. Carried to its extreme, the result can be the type of genocide practiced by Nazi Germany. Fortunately, eugenics lost much of its appeal following World War II, but not before it introduced the concept of selective sterilization to American society.

The positive social change that came along at about the same time was compulsory school attendance. By forcing every child to attain a certain amount of schooling, it created the need for special education to assist those mentally or physically unable to learn within the normal school environment.

By the end of World War I, according to the American Association for the Study of the Feeble-Minded, there were fifty-eight public facilities, and another eighty private ones, for the housing and care of people with intellectual disabilities. The population of the public institutions alone was just under 43,000. But this number was growing at an alarming rate. A dozen years earlier, a new classification system identifying degrees of disability had been formulated. A new term was being used to identify those on the moderate end of retardation. They were called "morons." Since this term also encompassed people who might have only mild learning disabilities, it swelled the total number of people considered disabled. This was coupled with another new belief: that

adults, particularly those with mild disabilities, were in reality a social menace.

One of the favored solutions with many professionals to deal with these alarming trends was forced sterilization. It was felt that this method would control behavior by keeping society's intellectually disabled from becoming sexual deviants as they matured, and that they could be safely paroled back into their community if they were not able to procreate. Sterilization could also manage "weak stock," since it was still believed that mental retardation was a hereditary aberration. A 1927 Supreme Court decision in favor of forced sterilization fueled the practice.

More than 60,000 young Americans, mostly poor, rural, white and uneducated, were forcibly sterilized. This figure does not include untold thousands of blacks and Native Americans whose sterilizations were not officially tracked. In all, thirty-five states participated in the practice.

Once again, it was Nazi Germany that opened the eyes of most people to the inherent dangers in forced sterilization. In 1934 the Nazis began what would eventually be the sterilization of 400,000 of their own people as part of their planned creation of a pure race. This coincided with a growing belief in a "new" psychiatry that placed an emphasis on mental hygiene, societal adaptation and community-based services to deal with the people with intellectual disabilities. Sterilization would not end completely, however; with the Great Depression, followed by World War II, parole into the community became more difficult, and once again warehousing became the primary function of the institutions. Forced sterilizations continued until the late 1970s or early 1980s.

At the end of World War II, newspapers and magazines began to run exposes of the terrible conditions in the public facilities for the mentally ill; and even workers within the system began to come forward with their own horrifying accounts, such as this 1946 letter by a twenty-eight-year old Quaker attendant:

> On this cold and wintry night there are 2,500 morons, imbeciles, and idiots asleep in the large brick buildings, which surround me. For the past eleven months I have worked here, at one time with a group of 130 morons of school age and at another time with thirty-three tubercular boys ranging from the lowest incontinent idiot to a moron who tinkers with a radio. . . . Conditioned thoroughly by a pattern of violence over a period of years, these defectives have nothing to look back on and less to hope for.

The late 1940s and early 1950s was also a period many scientists would like to forget. At their urging, the mentally retarded of this country were used as human guinea pigs to test the Salk poliovirus vaccine. Worse yet, they were fed radiation poisoning to test human reaction to that deadly killer.

As America entered the decade of the 1950s — a peaceful and a prosperous time for most of the nation's citizens — new writings about mental retardation began to emerge. Pearl S. Buck, winner of a Nobel Prize for literature, published *The Child Who Never Grew* in 1950. It is the heart wrenching tale of one mother's realization that her daughter was "different," how she came to accept it, and how she dealt with it. Buck's decision to have her ten-year old child institutionalized gave heart to thousands of other parents who had made the same decision. She counseled her readers that they should accept their child's condition, and keep them at home in their early years. Then, she wrote, " . . . in the best interest of the child, place them in an environment with their own kind."

Buck's book started a mini trend, and other parental confession books followed. Most psychiatrists of the era were still recommending institutionalization, so most of the authors of the books had followed that course, confident they had done the right thing for their child. But there was another opinion on the subject that was just beginning to be raised, and it took voice as well.

Roy Rogers and Dale Evans were one of the most respected couples in America in the early 1950s. They were both movie stars, with their clean cut images, good guys wear white and bad guys wear black cowboy movies, and gospel singing appearances. Being devout Christians, the two were featured in newspapers doing charity as often as making movies. Both had children from previous marriages, and they would adopt more children later. But their one natural child, a daughter named Robin born in 1950, had Down syndrome.

Robin would live for only two years, dying of mumps and encephalitis. Dale Evans eased her grief by writing of the child, and what she had meant to the Rogers' family during her brief stay on earth, in a small, poignant book, *Angel Unaware*. Unlike Buck and most other parents, the Rogers called Robin an angel sent from paradise, and said that all special children should be kept at home. Angels have a purpose that is lost in an institution, she believed:

> I believe with all my heart that God sent her on a two year mission to our household, to strengthen us spiritually and to draw us closer together in the knowledge and love and fellowship of God.

> It has been said that tragedy and sorrow never leave us when they find us. In this instance, both Roy and I are grateful to God for the privilege of learning some great lessons of truth through His tiny messenger, Robin Elizabeth Rogers.

Although Evans most certainly gained some converts, most parents still continued to institutionalize their children with intellectual disabilities; and most physicians still advised it as the soundest way to insure the child's future and the emotional well being of the remaining members of the family unit.

But another social phenomenon was just dawning that would have widespread and long lasting ramifications for the care of the mentally retarded. A national association had formed, the National Association for Retarded Children, or NARC. Dale Evans had pledged all the royalties from her book to the group, which got it off to a running start. In conjunction with the founding of the national group, local groups had also sprung up all around the country composed of parents of retarded children. They banded together for mutual support, for education, and most importantly, for demanding new community services for their children. By the end of the decade there would be nearly 600 local associations.

♥ ♥ ♥

The 1960s saw significant change in the treatment of the mentally retarded, according to Steven Noll and James W. Trent. Fueled by the scandals of the postwar years, the advocacy of President John F. Kennedy and his family, a greater public understanding of mental health, and a national awareness of civil rights, public policy began shifting throughout the 1960s and 1970s. Under pressure from President Kennedy, in October 1963 legislation was passed designed to encourage the establishment of more facilities for the retarded in all the states.

The state of Nevada was quick to respond. An executive committee composed of leading health officials was formed to study the issue; and throughout 1964 meetings were held to discuss the state's response to the new law. A report was finally issued proposing "the development of a comprehensive program for the mentally retarded in Nevada." Although much of the committee's work ended up as simply hollow rhetoric, some programs did finally begin to emerge.

By the mid 1970s, segregated public institutions and special classrooms lost favor with politicians, professionals and the public; and a radical policy shift toward mainstreaming and community integration of people with intellectual disabilities occurred.

Freed from the old stereotypes and restrictions, many of those labeled mentally retarded began to thrive in schools and workplaces across the nation. And finally, in 1990, the passage of the Americans with Disabilities Act once and for all prohibited discrimination against individuals with all disabilities, including mental retardation, in employment, public services and public accommodations.

The turnaround was not complete — there are many forms of discrimination that cannot be legislated — and it still is not, now early in the twenty-first century. But great and lasting strides had finally been made.

The famous mushroom cloud from an early 1950s atomic test outside Las Vegas.

CHAPTER THREE

The Beginning:
Who Will Help Our Children?

Mommy asked [the doctor] what she and Daddy should do. What did anyone do with a Mongoloid baby? Doctor said gently that there wasn't much anyone could do; the few institutions for such babies were overcrowded, and the state homes and hospitals wouldn't take in "one of these children" until she was four years old. Then he said something fine: "Take her home and love her. Love will help more than anything else in a situation like this — more than all the hospitals and all the medical science in the world." [Roy Rogers] was learning that it isn't really we innocent children who suffer, it's the ones around us who suffer . . .

— *Dale Evans Rogers,* Angel Unaware, *1953*

Las Vegas in the 1950s was driven by two industries: tourism (meaning gaming) and defense spending. The population had grown. Clark County's 1950 census showed 48,289 people, while the city of Las Vegas accounted for just above half of it, and new homes, shopping, and jobs were plentiful.

The decade saw new state and federal buildings joining the resort high rises, and Nellis Air Force Base was becoming a major military base, and a new kind of big spender for the city. The Nevada Test Site opened early in the decade, and the first atomic bomb was detonated.

The Strip, along Las Vegas Boulevard south of Sahara, was fast becoming the center of tourism and gaming of the Las Vegas of the 1950s. The Desert Inn, the Dunes, the Riviera, the Sands, the Sahara, the Tropicana and the Hacienda joined the older, smaller resorts on the old Los Angeles Highway, acting as a magnet for gamblers from around the world. The older downtown joints increased their gambling odds in order to compete with the flashier new resorts, and attracted a whole new generation of low-budget tourists to the city.

It was a grand time for all. Well, for most, perhaps.

Although the treatment of mental retardation was just beginning to emerge from its Dark Ages, it was still far from being progressive in the early 1950s. But a new and powerful force was at work. In communities all across the country, spearheaded by the parents of mentally retarded children, local support groups had been formed. For the first time, these groups were making their voices heard.

In the small desert community of Las Vegas, Nevada, and throughout the surrounding Clark County area, the same thing was happening. It started with one lonely voice, the voice of a small, unassuming woman in her early thirties named Dessie Bailey.

For Dessie and Al Bailey, there was never any serious thought of institutionalizing their little Claudia. We cannot know whether they had read Dale Evans Rogers' poignant story about keeping her daughter at home, but it is obvious that the Baileys agreed with that emerging notion. Even if they had considered sending Claudia away, their choices were few. Nevada had only one state hospital that provided custodial mental health care, and it was located in faraway Northern Nevada, in the small town of Sparks. It

wasn't that Nevada was insensitive to the issue, it was simply a matter of numbers. Nevada was the second least-populous state in the nation, followed only by Alaska. With only 160,083 people in the 1950 Census, Nevada trailed the next state up the list — tiny Delaware — by almost 250 percent.

It's true that California and other neighboring states offered a number of private facilities, but the costs were very high for working people like the Baileys. Still, according to one of Dessie Bailey's best friends, Florence Jones, the couple could have scraped together the money to send Claudia away had they wanted to do so. But, everything considered, it was an easy decision when they decided to care for Claudia themselves. However, that did not mean, by any stretch of the imagination, that Dessie Bailey was planning to sit back and accept whatever meager crumbs of assistance the state of Nevada, Clark County, or the city of Las Vegas, might dole out for her daughter's health and welfare.

♥ ♥ ♥

Those early years, when Claudia was an infant, were certainly not easy years, but at least the Baileys did not have to depend upon anyone else for the care and nurturing of their daughter. The family showered their little one with as much love and tenderness as they could muster. They had all her medical needs tended to, and watched her grow. The doctors had warned that Claudia might not ever walk on her own, but brother Pat recalls that she was walking by age two with no difficulty.

For many families with a disabled child in the early 1950s, the self-imposed isolation was one of the worst parts. The stigma of having such a child was a source of strain, and would keep to a minimum any interaction between the child and anyone else beyond the immediate family. For many parents, outright denial that they had a child with an intellectual disability was commonplace.

Even within the walls of their own homes, these families had to deal with new and frightening challenges. Siblings learned quickly that their needs were relegated to a secondary position. Though Al and Dessie Bailey shared the workload with Claudia, at least to the extent that Als' job would allow, in many families that was not the case. Often the brunt of the caregiving fell to one spouse, invariably the mother. For many, it was simply too much, and the decision to institutionalize the child would become the only sane option. But not for the Baileys.

" . . . I do remember there were times when I'd suddenly start to cry," Dessie Bailey once told a *Las Vegas Review-Journal* reporter. "Once when that happened," she continued, "I was doing the dishes and my son Pat, who was three at the time, walked in. He looked up at me and said, 'Don't cry, Momma. I'll take care of Claudia when you can't.'"

Never a procrastinator, she began searching the community for a school where Claudia's special needs could be served once she was old enough to begin attending. But it was a futile search; public schools were not required to serve children with severe intellectual or physical disabilities at the time. Though arguments before the United States Supreme Court in the case of Brown vs. the Board of Education — the

Al and Dessie Bailey with their son Patrick and daughter Claudia.

landmark school desegregation law — began in 1952, it would not be decided until 1954. In the meantime, southern lawyers argued that if the Supreme Court required them to serve African-Americans in the schools, it would only be a matter of time before they would be forced to serve disabled children too!

"I knew of two more [children with intellectual disabilites] here in Las Vegas," Bailey later wrote. "I asked around if there were any schools for such children. The answer was no."

But she was not easily deterred. The next couple of years would prove to be a period of highs and lows, of seeming victories that turned into hollow defeats, and of frustration, disappointment and anger. Parents of children with intellectual disabilities were not alone in their quest for help for their children. Parents of physically disabled children also saw their sons and daughters excluded from attendance at public schools.

The National Society for Crippled Children, now the National Easter Seal Society, is the granddaddy of support organizations for physically handicapped children. It was founded in 1921 in Ohio; and by the late 1940s the Society had chapters around the nation, including one in the Reno/Carson City area of northern Nevada. In 1949, hearing the pleas for help from their southern neighbors, the group from Reno/Carson City sent a team to Las Vegas to launch a chapter of the Society in the desert community.

Southern Nevada parents of children with disabilities immediately joined the local chapter, but according to Dessie Bailey, most of the early members were parents whose children had intellectual disabilites. A clinic was scheduled for the parents in the area, and Bailey, along with another parent, Mrs. Helen Dial, was asked to rally support for the clinic. They went to the Clark County Health Department and were given a list of names and addresses of families that had children with intellectual disabilities.

"Helen Dial and I worked together," she later wrote. "We were given a list of handicapped children, supposed to be living in Las Vegas. We were asked about going to their homes to see if they still lived there. Many doors were closed when we asked if such a child lived there — so we didn't do too good."

Regardless, Dessie Bailey, Helen Dial and a Mrs. Blackford took their children to the clinic on the assigned day. In a sad comment on the times, however, Bailey wrote, "Two of our children were turned away because they had Down syndrome. One of the doctors made fun of one," she sadly related. Writing later, she did soften her opinion of the organization somewhat, writing, "Today they do a lot of good for them," meaning for children with intellectual disabilities.

Frustrated, hurt, and angry, most of the parents pulled away from the Crippled Children's Society. But just as one door closed, another opened for the small band of parents. They formed their own private association, the Clark County School for the Handicapped, and Dessie Bailey was elected to the first board of directors. Word got out into the community about the group's plight, and a call came from an unlikely source: the hotel industry.

Helen Dial went to visit the El Rancho Vegas, the first major hotel/resort to be built on Las Vegas Boulevard back in 1941. There she met with the publicity manager of the hotel, Herb McDonald, and explained her group's aims and the obstacles they were facing. She asked for help, not just for the children with intellectual disabilities, but also for kids with physical disabilities. In one of those rare cases of all the stars becoming aligned at exactly the same moment in time, McDonald was excited by her visit.

He explained that a group of local hotel executives and entertainers had recently banded together to form a chapter of the Variety Club, a national organization of show business men dedicated to supporting children's charities in their communities. So far, McDonald confessed, they had not been granted a charter because they first had to line up a suitable charity to throw their support behind.

In that moment, a marriage was made. Variety Club was founded in Pittsburgh in 1927 by eleven young men in various branches of show business. It was originally planned as a social club. But their true calling came a year later, on Christmas Eve, when a baby girl was abandoned in the Sheridan Theater, which was managed by one of the young men. A note was pinned to the clothing of the foundling:

Please take care of my baby. Her name is Catherine. I can no longer take care of her. I have eight others. My husband is out of work. She was born on Thanksgiving Day. I have always heard of

But just as one door closed, another opened for the small band of parents.

the goodness of show business and I pray to God that you will look after her.

— A Heart-Broken Mother

The men accepted the plea. They acted as Catherine's godfathers, underwriting her support and education, and the group that today proclaims itself "The Children's Charity" had found its true purpose.

In 1950, the Las Vegas chapter of the Variety Club, Tent 39, was chartered. Chapters were called "tents" after the circus big top, while members were known as "barkers." The president was the Head Barker. Today, renamed Variety, the Children's Charity, this exceptional organization has more than ten thousand members and fifty-four chapters in fourteen countries.

Things began to happen quickly now. The parents of the children told the Variety Club members that their greatest need was for a school where their children's special needs could be met. Tent 39 swung into action. They informally adopted the group, and the parents began calling their group "The Buck-A-Month Club." Herb McDonald was named the president of the group.

Meanwhile, the Variety Club decided to put on a Big Show to raise money for the cause. Bob Cannon of the Buck-a-Month Club was appointed "doughboy," or ticket chairman; and all the parents helped sell tickets to the event. On a typically hot summer evening, on July 31, 1950, the first "Night of Stars" was held at the Last Frontier Hotel. It was a rousing success, according to the **Las Vegas Review-Journal's** August 1, 1950 edition:

"Night of Stars" Greatest Event Held in Vegas
The "Night of Stars" benefit sponsored by the Variety club of Las Vegas for the proposed School for Handicapped Children of Clark county, held last

A novel ad for the Night of Stars. Courtesy Variety, The Children's Charity.

night in the sports arena of the Hotel Last Frontier, raised approximately $10,000, all of which will be used toward establishment of the school.

It was the most successful show of its type ever staged in Las Vegas, and featured two and one half hours of entertainment presented by stars of the five resort hotels of Las Vegas, in addition to Dennis O'Keefe famous motion picture actor, and Eddie Bracken, comedian, who came to Las Vegas especially to participate in the benefit.

Miss Froman [singer Jane Froman] urged that everybody "give until it feels good" in the interest of the school for the unfortunate children of this area.

With funds now available to begin construction of the special school, land was needed. Dessie and Al Bailey made an appointment with Mayor Ernest "Ernie" Cragin, a pioneer businessman in the city.

Cragin was sensitive to their needs; and arranged to grant them a five-and-a-half acre parcel in back of the Sunrise School at 2601 Sunrise Avenue, just east of North Eastern Avenue near Fremont Street. It was a happy day for the group!

With the goal within their grasp, the parents began thinking about a teacher for the soon-to-be school. Helen Dial stepped forward again. In addition to having her teaching credentials, she had worked at the Tracy School for the Deaf in Los Angeles, so she was experienced working with special needs children. Dial secured the use of a room in the local Lutheran church and began working with a few of the mentally retarded children. Ground was broken on the Variety School for Handicapped Children. "All the heavy labor was volunteered, and most of the materials, such as ready-mix concrete and cinder blocks, were contributed by local businesses," Pat Bailey recalled.

"I and Mrs. Dial or Mr. Sanders would take food, coffee, etc," Dessie Bailey wrote. "I lived closer so I went most of the time. Sometimes we would pick up sandwiches from the hotels and coffee if it was a cold or rainy day."

Pat also remembers another contribution his mother made:

One of the things that my mother really knew how to do was to cook for a crowd. And one of the things that she really liked to cook was her own recipe for chili. Many chili purists will tell you that "There are no beans in chili, and no tomatoes either." Her chili contained both — and it was GOOOO–OOD! She'd whip up at least two or three big pots

of it every week and we'd run it over to the school as it was being built. Whenever we got there, it was lunchtime!

In June 1951 a second "Night of Stars" was held, and with 3,500 to 4,000 Las Vegans in attendance, another $10,000 was raised.

By the end of 1951, the school was finished. It had one very large classroom, a dining room or all-purpose room, a kitchen, four bathrooms, two offices, a speech room, a nurse's room and a large physical therapy room. To the members of the Buck-a-Month Club, it was the Taj Mahal.

Bailey's friend, Florence Jones, remembered the sad events that transpired next:

I sat with her [Dessie] on the board the night the decision was made on the category of children to be accepted for the first classes, starting in

Big Band leader Ted Lewis highlighted an early Variety Club Night of Stars event. Courtesy Variety, The Children's Charity.

1952. The decision was to enroll those physically handicapped and intellectually educable. Although this category excluded her own child, Dessie voted with the others on the Board, because this was progress toward education of children who previously had no chance. Dessie cherished education as others might cherish a fine painting.

Though brave and self-sacrificing on the outside, there is no question that Dessie and Al Bailey and the other parents of the more severely disabled children were devastated. Nobody had worked harder to make this first step possible than she, but now Claudia was again on the outside looking in. But Dessie Bailey was not a quitter. She was happy and excited for those who would attend the school, and more determined than ever to see that Claudia and other children like her would also have their day. She continued on the board as corresponding secretary, writing years later, "Ha ha — couldn't type, but I got action!"

January 5, 1952, was a historical day in Las Vegas. Fourteen physically handicapped children attended their first day of school in the brand new Variety School for Handicapped Children. This was the first time for many of these children to be in contact with other children like themselves. It was also the first time most of them had been away from their parents, attending the four-hour school day. It was also a first

Variety Club's Head Barker (president) assists disabled children at the new Variety School for Handicapped Children.

for the state of Nevada: the first school for children with disabilities in the state.

Variety Clubs, which had made it all possible, scheduled their sixteenth annual convention to be held in Las Vegas in 1952, with over one thousand show business performers and business leaders set to attend. It was one of the largest conventions to date in the city that would eventually become the convention capital of the world.

Variety Clubs International held their 1952 convention in Las Vegas, and attended the ceremonial opening of their namesake school, the first in Nevada for handicapped children. Courtesy Variety, The Children's Charity.

The first event on the group's schedule was the official dedication and ribbon cutting for the Variety School for Handicapped Children. Over three hundred conventioneers attended, along with a crowd of locals. "The school is expected to be one of the finest in the southwest," the *Las Vegas Review-Journal* said, in reporting on the dedication.

A "Handbook of Information," published by the school for the 1952–1953 academic year, provides a great deal of detailed information about the landmark school. Mrs. Helen Welborn was the first acting principal, and doubled as the speech therapist. In addition to teachers, there was also a dietitian and a registered nurse. A consulting orthopedist, pediatrician and physical therapist were also on call.

A special committee, named The School for Handicapped Children Committee, was formed from within the parental group, and the school principal answered directly to this committee. The school's underlying management philosophy stated, "In this school, there are no bosses — we are all coworkers."

Dessie Bailey and the other parents, having had their disabled children excluded from the new Variety School, picked up their campaign once again. Bailey prodded parents of other disabled children in the city, and made personal visits to almost every city and county official who would open their door for her.

In 1953 the Las Vegas Union School District voted to incorporate the Variety Club School into its district, taking advantage of some additional state funds the legislature had set aside for the purpose. The school was renamed Variety School for Special Education, and a small crack opened in the door for the Baileys and other parents.

A 1974 newspaper interview with Dessie Bailey in the *Las Vegas Review-Journal* reported what happened next:

In 1953 Dessie had a nervous breakdown. Her body, her mind and her heart said "no more." Claudia now age five was put into a private boarding arrangement in California with 80 other children having the same problems as she. For 18 months Dessie visited her little girl who never forgot the family while they all grew and strengthened, mentally and physically to begin anew. When Claudia came home it was apparent she had learned and enjoyed being with her peers.

Despite her illness, Dessie Bailey's dream for her daughter's future never wavered. As she rested her body, her mind was still focused on the dream. She polished it. She burnished it. Then finally, she placed it quietly away where it could be quickly recalled when she was completely mended.

Tommy Wilcox, one of Opportunity Village's original adult clients, refinishes a chair in this photo from the early 1970s.

The Early Struggles:
You Win Some, You Lose Some

When she was strong again, even while Claudia was still in California, Dessie Bailey began anew. She again pleaded with other parents to join her in the struggle for their mentally challenged children. Claudia was now of school age, so, if anything, Bailey actually increased the tempo of her unflagging campaign. Finally, in March 1954, she made a major breakthrough.

Al and Dessie were joined in their living room by five other individuals or sets of parents they had recruited to the cause. These six formed Clark County Association for Retarded Children (CCARC), and the group was formally chartered by the State of Nevada in July. Three years later it would be granted a charter as an official chapter of the National Association for Retarded Children.

The *Las Vegas Review-Journal* reported the outcome of the Saturday meeting in Monday's edition:

An organization to assist in the general welfare of retarded children has been organized by a group of local citizens who call themselves "The Clark County Association for Retarded Children."

The purpose of the group, which was organized Saturday night, is to try to establish a residential school for retarded children.

The group figures it will be necessary to raise $5,000 to get the school underway, and is currently working on a plan to raise the amount through a loan which would be repaid by tuition in several years.

The group estimates there are 40 to 50 retarded children in the Las Vegas area which would benefit by the school. Teachers for the school would be provided by a California concern.

Officers of the group elected Saturday night are Walter Grundy, president; Ina Gragson, first vice-president; Ralph Steiner, second vice-president; Mrs. Carlyle Wilcox, Treasurer; Dessie Bailey, corresponding secretary; Elbert Bailey, membership chairman; and Helen Dial, public relations. Additional directors named were Carlyle Wilcox, Mrs. William Acklin and Alta Staton.

Eight names actually appeared on the original charter, representing six individual or sets of parents. These six individuals or couples, recognized as the official charter members of what would eventually become Opportunity Village, were: Dessie and Al Bailey, Mary and Ralph Steiner, Helen Dial, Ina Gragson, Walter J. Grundy, and Jesma Wilcox. There were other parents who were also involved from the very beginning, but had not attended the meeting at the Bailey's house, so there was a solid core group of concerned parents to rely on.

The founders were a diverse group. The one thing that bound them all together was that each had a retarded child that nobody seemed to want to help. So they would help and support each other.

In the Gragson family, Ina Gragson carried most of the load with their Down syndrome daughter, Inantha. Her husband Robert, known as "Blackie" to friends, was a heavy equipment mechanic, a job that kept him on the road throughout the state much of the time. But whenever he was home, Blackie Gragson was right there working with the other parents. His brother, Oran Gragson, was the mayor of Las Vegas from 1959 until 1975. The Gragsons lived on Maryland Parkway.

Helen Dial had become one of Dessie Bailey's best friends as they fought for their children's rights. Helen and Arthur Dial lived on North 25th Street, not far from where the Variety School was eventually built. They had two young sons, and one, Artie, was moderately disabled. Artie died sometime in the early to mid 1950s, but Helen Dial carried on alone, being very active in CCARC. She was a teacher, and served as the very first teacher for the children with disabilities while the Variety School was being built. Dial eventually remarried and moved to Southern California, where she died around 1980.

Very little is recalled of Ralph Grundy, who did not remain active in CCARC for too many years. The Grundy's lived on South Third Street, in a house with a large screened-in porch, and Pat Bailey remembered that Mrs. Grundy "made the best lemonade in the world!" The Grundys daughter, Carol, appears to have passed away early in the history of CCARC, and Ralph

Grundy was forced to resign the presidency in the summer of 1954 due to his ill health.

Jesma and Carlyle Wilcox were Nevada pioneers. Jesma Wilcox was born in the small mining town of Delamar, Nevada, now a ghost town near Alamo, in 1903. As a baby, she traveled with her parents by horse-drawn wagon to the tiny railroad watering stop called Las Vegas to attend the 1905 land auction that marked the birth of the city. The family did not buy a lot. Instead, they moved to the small desert town of Panaca where Jesma grew up. In 1923 she married longtime Southern Nevada schoolteacher and principal, Carlyle Wilcox; and the couple moved to Las Vegas in 1942.

They leased the old Helen J. Stewart Ranch, which had been in existence even before the town began, and operated a public swimming pool and gift shop on the property. It was known as the Old Ranch swimming pool, and was one of only two public pools in town. Their son Tommy, born in 1945, had Down syndrome, but he is remembered as a happy, carefree boy who loved to play basketball. Carlyle Wilcox became the second president of CCARC, replacing Ralph Grundy when he resigned.

In 2006, Tommy, now Thomas, Wilcox was still an Opportunity Village client, one of the organization's oldest and most stable citizens at 60 years old. Jesma Wilcox died at 98 years old in 2002, the last of Opportunity Village's charter members.

Jesma and Carlyle Wilcox were two founding members of Clark County Association for Retarded Children the forerunner of Opportunity Village.

The last two founding members were Mary and Ralph Steiner. The Steiners had a son, Tom, with intellectual disabilities. No further information about the Steiners seems to be available, and none of the old-time CCARC members can recall any details about the family.

The stated goal for the fledgling organization was simple and to the point: to start a school for the children of Clark County who were mentally disabled. The group was unsure how much, if any, support they would be able to garner from city, county, or state government; but in truth, that didn't matter. They would have their school, and if they had to do it all by themselves, so be it.

♥ ♥ ♥

To understand the plight of these parents, one has to understand the history of public education in Nevada. Shortly after Las Vegas was born in 1905 with the railroad's land auction, the few permanent residents began to think about schooling for their children, and for the children of all the new people they were convinced would soon join them. The first plan called for constructing a frame school building on the southwest corner of Second and Lewis, and land had been put aside for the purpose, so it was purchased. But it was soon learned that the old Salt Lake Hotel, just down the dusty road, was for sale at a bargain price. The *Las Vegas Age* reported what happened.

The two rooms were finished in cloth and paper with a patch board ceiling, and a pot-bellied stove

The old Salt Lake Hotel, with the belfry added later, became the nascent city's first school in 1905. Inset is the first class and teachers.

SCHOOL HOUSE

Trustees Purchase Old Salt Lake Hotel Building

Supt. of Schools Sanders and Trustee Lake have negotiated the purchase of the old Salt Lake Hotel building and will convert it into a school house.

The building will be moved at once to the school site, corner Second and Lewis streets, and put in proper condition. It is 40x48 feet in size and will be divided into two large rooms.

The building was bought for $150 and can be roofed and put in shape for $555. The price of the new building contemplated by the trustees was $1170. Thus a saving of about $450 is effected by the new deal.

was added. The building was ready to accept its first students on October 2nd; and eighty-one children enrolled, immediately swamping the space in the old converted hotel. By the next month, enrollment had swelled to 114 children, and a tent had been erected on the property to handle the overflow. Despite the crowded conditions, Sophia Schultz and Alma Tuttle, the town's first teachers, carried on as best they could.

The first graduating class, from the eighth grade, was held in 1907, with Julia Westlake, Frank Ferris and Thomas Lake getting their diplomas. In 1910 the clapboard school burned down, and was replaced the following year with the town's first permanent school, a large two-story building that was shared by Clark County High School and Las Vegas Grammar School. Public education in Southern Nevada was off and running, but, like cities and towns across the nation, only for physically fit and intellectully apt students.

♥ ♥ ♥

By the early 1950s, public education was in a state of crisis in Nevada, but even more so in Southern Nevada and its largest county, Clark County. Because Clark County was so isolated, and had always been less populated than Northern Nevada's Washoe County, home of Reno and the state capital in Carson City, it had always been relegated to step-child status in state affairs. The 1950 census showed that Clark County had quickly been gaining ground, however, and trailed Washoe County by only 2,200 people. By 1954 it had passed its rival, and by the 1960 cen-

sus its population eclipsed its northern counterpart by more than fifty percent.

Still, the same political mindset prevailed. In fact, most historians believe that Southern Nevada's unparalleled growth was viewed with alarm in the north. Northern counties and their politicians saw the south as a growing threat to their domination of the state.

In 1953, due to its growth and the under-funding of its schools by the state, Clark County was forced to put many children on half days, and crowd others into abandoned army barracks. The following year, when enrollment swelled by twenty-six percent in one year, the governor was forced to call a special session of the legislature and allocate money from the general fund to keep the county's schools open.

Matt Kelly's school band, around 1917, at Las Vegas' first permanent school building. It was shared by Las Vegas Grammar School and Clark County High School. Photograph Courtesy of Elbert Edwards Collection, University of Nevada, Las Vegas Library.

Southern Nevada's growth however, was only part of the problem. Even without growth, the state simply had not allocated enough money to education. Thus, by 1955 even the northern schools began to have funding problems, and that fact finally convinced legislators that there simply wasn't enough money available for the task. So in 1956, after a lot of study and gnashing of political teeth, Nevada consolidated its 208 elementary and high school districts into seventeen county school districts.

R. Guild Gray was the superintendent of Las Vegas Union School District Number 2 at the time, a position he had held since 1953. He became the first superintendent of the Clark County School District, a position he held until 1961.

Gray was the quintessential Nevadan. Born in Peoria, Illinois, his parents brought him to the state when he was only two years old. He was raised in Reno, schooled at the University of Nevada, and received advanced degrees in education at Stanford University and the University of Southern California. His lifelong love of the state came as a result of his many years of wandering the mountains and deserts of Nevada as an educator, businessman and politician of the state he had adopted. After retirement he continued to explore all the rural nooks and crannies of The Silver State, and became a respected poet, writer, photographer and historian of all things Nevada. Gray died in 1998.

At the same time school consolidation had been legislated, a sales tax had been enacted to assist educa-

R. Guild Gray was the first Superintendent of the newly reorganized Clark County School District. He served from 1956 until 1961. Photograph Courtesy of Southern Nevada Educators Collection, University of Nevada, Las Vegas Library.

tion, and state aid increased. But Clark County's problems were not over; it still faced the difficult task of consolidating its fourteen school districts with over 20,000 children scattered over 8,000 square miles.

Gray's newly consolidated school district began with an aggregate enrollment of 20,420 children. An interesting sidelight to the Clark County School District reorganization was a list of "Guiding Principles" that were drafted, upon which educational policy would be based. Principle number one stated that the board of education and its staff were charged, "To provide every public school child in the county, regardless of place of residence, an educational program equal to the best which can be found in a comparable environmental situation."

This must have sounded like heavenly music to the ears of the families with whose children had disabilities. But Gray, writing his Stanford University PhD dissertation on the formation of the Clark County School District a few years later, said otherwise:

> Guiding Principle number one, though it recognized the rights of every child in the County . . . did not throw open the doors of opportunity so wide that the new district was obligated to provide the same for all children. "Environmental situation" was the key phrase in the statement.

Although Gray did not go on to spell out which groups were excluded by "environmental situation," children with intellectual disabilities certainly were.

They were never considered in any of the new state legislation or reorganization.

♥ ♥ ♥

So during the entire time the parents were fighting for school rights for their children, they were fighting an uphill battle. The schools did not have enough money to operate, even without considering special education. With growth factored into the equation, the problem became even more acute. On top of that, the school system was bogged down in consolidating fourteen systems into one.

Finally, even if all these problems could have been easily solved, the education of mentally retarded children was not even on the radar.

Realizing all these things, and recognizing that they would have to provide their own solutions, the newly formed CCARC was moving forward. One of the men in attendance at the meeting in Al and Dessie's living room that evening was Peter Updike. Updike owned and operated a school for children with intellectual disabilities in Colton, California, and Dessie Bailey had convinced him to consider opening a similar facility in Las Vegas. Updike had agreed, and now he began putting the wheels in motion.

He rented a brand new building at 310 North Ninth Street, and named it the Updike School. Joyce Creiger and May E. Perrin were hired as the first two teachers. Finally, in December 1954 the school opened its doors to what would eventually become twenty-seven children with intellectual disabilities. Seven-year old Claudia Bailey was a happy member of the first class.

Parents paid $100 a month to send their children to the Updike School, and had to provide their own transportation to and from the school. Still, it seemed like a godsend to them. Dessie Bailey's dream, it appeared, had finally come true.

Like most dreams, this one was fleeting. After only one year of operation, in December 1955, Peter

Children with intellectual disabilities attend the first class at the private Updike School, which would fail after only one year.

A 1956 photo of a teacher and her students at the Updike School for the mentally retarded.

Updike was forced to close the school due to lack of funds. The parents, however, were not ready to give up.

There were a few students in the school from the city of Henderson, to the southeast of Las Vegas. Henderson had been born during World War II, when the Basic Magnesium, Inc. plant opened to supply the War Department with magnesium for munitions and airplane parts. By 1947, however, production had ended and most of the plant's 14,000 workers had moved on. Many of the townsite houses and buildings were left vacant; and the federal government was actually poised to offer Henderson for sale as war surplus property. The state moved to buy up the land, and saved it from its ignominious fate; and in 1953 the City of Henderson was incorporated with a population of 7,410 people.

Because Henderson rents were so cheap, the Henderson parents from the defunct Updike School convinced the CCARC to rent a building in the city and restart the school themselves. It turned out better than they had anticipated. An empty building in one of Henderson's few public parks, Carver Park, was offered to the group rent free. It was an old facility but suitable, with two large rooms for classes, two bathrooms, a room for naps, and a spacious, fenced backyard for the children to play in. The Henderson schools donated some desks and cots, and a private donor gave a piano, some books and blackboards. The parents cleaned and repaired the building, and the school opened on Valentine's Day, 1956, with thirty children in attendance.

Two teachers had been found, both pensioners, and they accepted the jobs for a small salary. The remaining costs were paid through donations and an $80

The parents, however, were not ready to give up.

per month tuition. Bus transportation was arranged through the Tonopah-Reno Stage Line, an intercity bus line that traveled between Nevada and Arizona. Once again, the parents crossed their fingers.

But their luck didn't change. As they strove to find financial backing for the new school, Dessie Bailey wrote to the Nevada State Department of Health. On July 23, 1956, she received a response:

Nevada has never had a program for the child with intellectual disabilities that was supported by state and Federal funds. Until recently (approximately two years ago) there was no special resource in the state for the retarded child outside of the State Hospital [in Sparks.] Since then a number of local school systems in the state have become interested in the problem using local and state education funds which can be used for that purpose but are not earmarked for special classes for the retarded.

The letter went on to cite a few examples in the state where the new county school districts had indeed allocated funds for special education classes. It became obvious that money might be available, but it would have to be squeezed like blood from a turnip from the fledgling Clark County School District. A second letter arrived only two weeks later from United States Senator Alan Bible of Nevada informing the CCARC that as a private organization they would not be eligible for any type of financial aid from public funds, state or federal.

There were, however, a few small rays of hope at about the same time. In September 1956 the school closed down for a month while the two teachers studied for and received their Nevada teaching certification. That accomplished, the new Clark County

School District agreed to pick up the cost of their salaries, relieving the parents of that burden. And in November, the Variety Club donated a bus to CCARC for transportation. Al Bailey and two firemen alternated driving the bus on their days off to and from Henderson. Due to these two boons, tuition fees were lowered to $75 a month, then down to $55.

While the group was still reveling in the good news, and attempting to absorb all the bad news, they received the final blow. Another letter from the state informed them that their school was operating illegally, according to state education laws, and had to be closed. Thus, having been denied help from both the federal and state governments, and now disallowed from helping themselves, the CCARC shut down the Henderson School for Retarded Children after only eighteen months of operation.

It had not all been in vain. The voices that had spoken so long and so eloquently had finally been heard. Years later, Dessie Bailey said of the struggle:

> By this time, we had been fighting with the school board to let us put the children in the Variety School. We kept fighting them until they gave in. On September 27, they allowed us to put them in. I always wondered why they were so narrow-minded about it. We just wanted to show the public and the school board that it could be done, that it was feasible and it wouldn't cost that much.

The Clark County School District allocated some additional funds to the Variety School for Special Education in October 1957. Four rooms were added to the school, and thirty children with intellectual disabilities became part of the public school system for the first time.

The CCARC had won a huge victory.

The next few years were full of new challenges, some defeats and a few victories. After only a short

time, the school district also began accepting children with behavioral and psychological disorders into the new rooms at Variety School. After an attempt to combine the two groups failed, these children were assigned two of the four new rooms at Variety School. Overcrowding for both groups was commonplace, and half-day session had to be inaugurated so every child could be served. Disappointed parents saw the service as little more than a part time babysitting function rather than an educational opportunity.

All that started to change in 1958 when Howard Marr, an experienced school administrator from Pennsylvania, moved to Las Vegas to become principal of the Variety School. Despite all the other problems that beset the CCARC and its parents, this proved to be one of the best things that ever happened to education for the handicapped in Clark County. Marr was a natural born leader, and his understanding of, and dedication to, the cause of the handicapped soon lead to his being referred to by parents as "Mr. Special Ed."

> Dessie Bailey wrote of her friend some years later: He was a well trained man of special education who knew what and how to teach and handle all handicapped children, whether crippled or mentally retarded. The School Board was planning on doing away with the retarded children's classes, but Mr. Marr said a firm "NO!" to this. This incident and many others in which he has stood his ground in the face of opposition have endeared him to all us parents . . . With his services, we as a group and the Variety Club have been able to say that we have one of the top Special Educators in the USA."

The state also finally earmarked some funds for special education just for children with intellectual disabilities, initially $200 per child per year, but increased by the end of the decade to $500. The

CCARC decided to hold a fundraising drive to augment the insufficient funds, but the Variety Club objected, saying that it would harm their annual drive, so the plan was abandoned. But rummage sales were held often to pay for needed furnishings and supplies.

The Variety School has gone on to achieve a long and distinguished record in serving Clark County's handicapped children. In 1976 an eight classroom addition was approved for the school. Fittingly, the new wing was named the Dessie Bailey Wing.

Today, Variety School serves children with disabilities, ages three to twenty-two, with totally individualized educational programs. It is one of three schools in Clark County devoted exclusively to disabled students. The others are the Helen J. Stewart School and the John F. Miller School.

VARIETY

BULLDOGS

VARIETY SCHOOL FOR SPECIAL EDUCATION
CLARK COUNTY SCHOOL DISTRICT
2601 East Sunrise Avenue
Las Vegas, Nevada 89101

Telephone 384-2393

Howard J. Marr, Principal
Carol Menninger, Coordinator
Homebound Instruction
Ron Stepke
Parent & Student Advisor

November 7, 1977

Mr. and Mrs. Robert Cannon
608 Kenny Way
Las Vegas, Nevada 89107

Dear Mr. and Mrs. Cannon:

You are cordially invited to attend the dedication of Variety School's newest classroom wing to Dessie Bailey, a charter founder and ardent supporter of Variety School. Ceremonies will occur at Variety School the evening of November 15th as part of our P.T.A. Meeting, which begins at 7:30 p.m. and ends at 8:30 p.m.

We are very proud of this latest addition to our campus. The new wing is composed of eight classrooms used for the education of the mentally retarded/multiply handicapped. We feel this dedication is a fitting tribute to Mrs. Bailey's years of service and efforts on our behalf. Please join her in making this an occasion Dessie will never forget.

Sincerely,

Howard J. Marr

Howard J. Marr

HJM:lp

R.S.V.P. - 384-2393

SERVING THE HANDICAPPED GRADES K-12

The Variety School invited community leaders to attend the dedication of the Dessie Bailey wing, which added eight classrooms to the school.

CHAPTER FIVE

Opportunity Village:
The Birth of a Legacy

Almighty and merciful God, we who are the parents and friends of the least of Your little ones, ask guidance and help in our efforts to brighten their lives, that we will become reconciled to their affliction. Grant that we may not despair as those who have no hope, but rather give us the grace to know Your wisdom and the courage to accept it nobly.
—Amen

— The official prayer of the National Association of Retarded Children, 1967

In 1961, a new group, calling themselves the Lake Mead Association for Retarded Children, sprang up, and sapped many members from the CCARC. The following year, Dessie Bailey was elected president of the smaller organization. Since beginning her solo campaign for people with intellectual disabilities more than a decade earlier, she was always most comfortable accepting only a supporting role. But when Variety School had formed its first PTA in the late 1950s, she had served two terms as president of that organization, and she discovered how much more she could accomplish if she was at the helm.

Having won the school fight, the CCARC parents now turned their thoughts to how the retarded could be served once they left school. With the same focused dedication and single mindedness that had carried the group so far, they carried their campaign for the mentally retarded to a whole new level.

As president, Bailey immediately established CCARC's first budget. It was readily apparent that the numbers on the "expense" side of the ledger were greater than the ones on the "income" side; and she knew something had to be done. Fundraisers were not possible because of the conflict with Variety Club; so she cast about for another idea. And at some point, it hit her — the **big** idea — and at that moment, the North Las Vegas Thrift Shop was born.

The depleted membership loved the idea, and everyone pitched in to make it a reality. "I took the chairmanship myself," Bailey later wrote, "because after seeing other presidents appoint committees only to have them fail to fulfill their jobs or finish a project, I thought it would be wise to see it through the first year myself." Wise indeed; history had proven that any task Dessie Bailey took on for the cause of the children simply could not — dared not — fail.

Somewhere during this period — perhaps before the thrift shop was opened, perhaps soon thereafter — CCARC did hold a fund-raising event to help finance the effort. The state PTA was scheduled to hold their annual convention in Las Vegas. The Carpenters' Union Hall was donated for the evening, a buffet dinner donated by Bob & Pearl's Supper Club, and beer and soda donated by an anonymous company. After a great evening of fun and celebration,

$177.50 had been raised to help furnish and stock the thrift shop building in North Las Vegas.

Pat Bailey remembered the early days of the thrift shop:

Somebody donated a two-room cinderblock building . . . Somehow entertainers from out on the Strip got word of it, and began donating some suits, dresses, shoes and such that had been worn maybe once or twice. I got to meet some of the people I'd only seen on black and white television: Jack Benny and Mary Livingston, Mssrs. Bud Abbott and Lou Costello, Louis Prima and Keely Smith (who also bought some of the Christmas cards I was selling!) — the list goes on.

My Dad's truck was kept busy shuttling donations from the Strip and other places out to NLV to the shop, where folks were buying it as fast as we could get it on the racks! When Dad had to quit having this much fun so he could go to work, one of the other fathers would load me up in his truck and we'd do the same thing. Fortunately, I was a good student, so my school work didn't suffer too badly.

Somehow entertainers from out on the Strip got word of it, and began donating some suits, dresses, shoes and such . . .

The store officially opened on June 6, 1962. It was manned entirely by volunteers, mostly families and friends of CCARC. First year's receipts for the enterprise totaled $10,625, an overwhelming success by every standard. The store continued to succeed for two more years, and a store manager was eventually hired. But then sales began to fall off, and the store was soon forced to close. A second store was opened, but it too failed after only a short time. It became obvious that the thrift

Parents prepare the organization's first thrift shop in North Las Vegas for its opening in 1962.

store had run its course, but no matter, a significant amount of cash had been raised toward the final goal: a training center for people with intellectual disabilites once they left the school system. For that purpose, it had been an unqualified success.

While the thrift store was running its course, and adding money to the treasury, CCARC was moving forward on establishing a vocational training center. Their first facility was a building at 918 South Fourth Street loaned to the group by the Kaltenborn family. The group began a sheltered workshop there in 1964. CCARC member Helen Dial suggested the name Opportunity Center, and it stuck. Later, a facility further south on Charleston Boulevard was opened to augment the Fourth Street location.

Opportunity Village officials realized, however, that the two location were only a temporary fix. Clark County's expanding adult population with disabilites could not be served indefinitely without entirely new,

enlarged facilities. To address the problem, CCARC appointed a land committee, and Joylin Vandenberg was appointed chair.

Vandenberg and her husband Rick, longtime Las Vegans, had a daughter, Valerie, about age eleven by this time, and had been active in the CCARC from the beginning. She was also the chairperson of the group's Opportunity Center. Vandenberg had heard that the federal government's Bureau of Land Management (BLM), which at the time owned more than ninety percent of all the real estate in Nevada, had land available for non-profit groups, and she filed an application to see if CCARC would qualify.

Qualify they did, and in 1965, BLM granted the organization a two-and-a-half acre withdrawal claim against an eighty acre parcel of land on west Charleston and Jones boulevards.

The next year, the state of Nevada began seeking a site for a comprehensive mental health center they planned to build. CCARC officials heard of the search and alerted the state planning board to the availability of the eighty acres. Soon the state entered into negotiations with BLM. CCARC was asked if it would surrender its withdrawal claim in return for a promise that its parcel would be deeded back after the deal with BLM was complete. They agreed. The state finalized the transfer of land from BLM and, good to their word, awarded CCARC a deed to their two-and-a-half acre parcel.

It appeared to be a good deal for everyone. The state could begin planning for their mental health center, and CCARC knew it would have a central location to build their new facilities when the time was right. Over the next few years they were promised that more land would be made available to them if and when they needed it.

History should have warned CCARC officials that it would not be that easy. However, they had been dis-

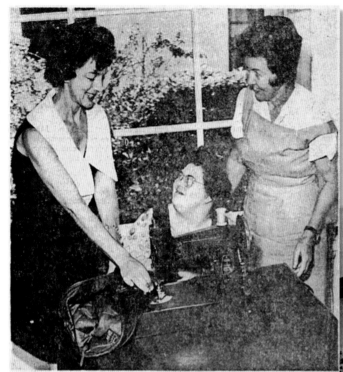

BUSY FINGERS

Mrs. Richard Vandenburg, Opportunity Center Committee chairman shows Inantha Gragson and Mrs. Helen Dial, director of the center, a sewing machine donated to the Opportunity Center. The two groups of retarded children have an Opportunity Pay Roll Time Card where they keep track of contracted jobs and receive bi-monthly checks.

Above: Joylin Vandenberg (left) and Helen Dial teach client Inantha Gragson how to use CCARC's new sewing machine in this early 1960s article. Right: The very first Retarded Children's Opportunity Center was located at 918 South Fourth Street.

THIS OLD HOUSE

This old house is 30 years old but its rooms are filled with happiness and the sound of children's laughter and conversations. It is the new Retarded Children's Opportunity Center located in Las Vegas at 918 South Fourth Street. An anonymous donor made the house and lot available to Clark County Association for retarded children at no cost.

a local attorney and ex-Air Force fighter pilot, who would go on to become the chief judge of the United States Federal District Court for Nevada. George, a lifelong Las Vegan, and his wife LaPrele also had a son, Dougie, with intellectual disabilities. The two businessmen realized that CCARC had reached a point where professional management was needed if the organization was to meet the challenges it

appointed so many times before that they could not help but feel that things were finally going their way. Instead, they would eventually find themselves in the midst of a political brouhaha that was to threaten the organization's very existence.

♥ ♥ ♥

By the late 1960s, some positive things began to happen for CCARC. Walter "Walt" Epprecht, a local Dodge dealer in Las Vegas and the parent of a son with intellectual disabilities, had been appointed president of CCARC. His vice president was Lloyd D. George,

faced. Some of the older members, including Dessie Bailey, opposed the move, fearing the costs would be too high. They also remembered how the thrift shop had failed after it was turned over to professional management. But the majority of CCARC members backed Epprecht and George, and their search began.

Like thousands of other unhappily married people over the years, Dr. Ted Johnson had come to Las Vegas for a "quickie" divorce. "I'd been separated for over two years," he told a *Las Vegas Sun* reporter in a 1972 interview. "But I figured while I was here I would

HEART AWARD DINNER - - - -

SPECIAL GUESTS — Special guests of Variety Tent, hotel officials and members who were present at the February 14 Award Dinner were: standing, from left, Barker for the evening Ivan Annenberg; Charlie Harrison, executive vice president of the Riviera; and Len Paves, hotel catering manager. They are shown greeting Mrs. Fay Zesblum, room mother; Heart Fund children Patricia Trafton and Kent Foster; and Mrs. Irene Parker, teacher's aide.

MRS. ELBERT BAILEY, founder of the Clark County School for Retarded Children, receives the Variety Club's 1967 Heart Award from Attorney Robert Jones at the Variety Club's annual Heart Award Dinner at the Riviera Hotel Tuesday, February 14th. This award is made to an individual in our community for their outstanding work and dedication in assisting handicapped and underprivileged children.

400 Members And Friends Fill Riviera Convention Hall

MRS. ELBERT BAILEY RECEIVES ANNUAL HEART AWARD HONOR

Before a gathering of more than 400 friends and neighbors, Mrs. Elbert (Dessie) Bailey was duly honored by members of Variety Club Tent 39 when they named her the recipient of the 1967 Heart Award.

Only one other woman (Sister Charles) was ever so honored. Amidst applause and cheers, Attorney Robert Jones warmly congratulates Mrs. Bailey as he handed her the Heart Plaque which signified the recognition of her outstanding work and long dedication in assisting handicapped and underprivileged children.

While the dinner and dancing was taking place in the Riviera Hotel Convention Hall, a group of children from the School for Special Education were enjoying the singing of Tony Martin in the Hotel's theatre dinning room as guests of the Hotel management.

The traditional Barker, who makes his appearance annually at the Heart Award dinner in full regalia, was portrayed this year by Press Guy Ivan Annenberg.

do volunteer work and found they were … thinking about hiring an executive director. I had been an executive director of the Pittsburgh, Pennsyvania, Association for Retarded Children for eight years, so I said, 'Well, if you've been thinking about it, there's no time like the present because I'm available and cheap.'"

Ted Johnson, the first fulltime professional administrator at the Clark County Association for Retarded Children.

"Dr. Johnson, we don't have much of a payroll," Lloyd George recalls telling him. "We don't know if we can pay you if you take this job."

"Don't worry about pay," Johnson told them. "If you hire me I guarantee that I'll be paid. I know how to run an operation like this."

Longtime Opportunity Village insiders swear to this day that as one marriage was being dissolved, another began. Epprecht and George hired Johnson in 1967, and neither he nor the organization ever looked back. "Without him, we wouldn't have grown as we did," Joylin Vandenberg recalled. Lloyd George agreed. "Ted made this thing happen very quickly," he said. "He just had the vision."

Johnson had a doctorate in education from Columbia University, and was an assistant professor at the University of Buffalo when his first son, Teddy, was born with severe intellectual disabilities. Like many parents at the time, Ted had gone through the shock, denial, and shame phases. But soon he began to do volunteer work. Eventually he decided to devote his professional life to working with people with intellectual disabilities after completing post doctoral work in special education at George Peabody College.

Little did he know when he came to Las Vegas to obtain a divorce how badly he was needed in the community. "When I first came," he told the *Las Vegas Sun* in 1973, "they had volunteers running their small program with a few people working part time. Our operating budget … was $8,000. Now [in 1973] our yearly operating budget is $400,000."

When Johnson accepted the position as executive director, there were nearly 750 children with intellectual disabilities in the Clark County School District. Eventually every one of them, upon turning eighteen, would be turned back into the community, joining thousands of others who were already languishing within the population. Ted Johnson realized his most important task was to see that there would be someplace for them to go when that happened. He set up shop in an upstairs office on Fremont Street, volunteered by the Georges, and began to work.

A significant breakthrough occurred in 1969 when for the first time CCARC was accepted into the United Fund, the forerunner of United Way. It received $48,212 toward its annual budget of $170,002 in that first year. Also, the state of Nevada gave a one-time $60,000 grant to the agency. The CCARC had to raise the remainder of their operating capital, and was well on its way to developing the self-sustaining ethic that makes it so unique today.

The organization's multi-faceted program, designed by Johnson, by this time included day care, vocational rehabilitation, camping, recreation, family counseling, public education, retailing, and community planning. The Variety School, and the newer Helen J. Stewart School, established in 1963, were finally doing a good job of educating the area's school age children with intellectual disabilities; so CCARC's mission had gravitated toward serving those outside the school system. It was developing into an efficient, across the board level of service for the growing population of Clark County's citizens with mental retardation.

In the late 1960s the group bought a property at 927 South Main Street, to which they soon added two other adjoining properties. Dr. Johnson explained that the purpose of the new center was to "expand the vocational and social life of anyone who is prevented from doing so normally." The center was divided into a number of rooms where various phases of rehabilitation could be conducted by trained professionals: physical therapy, dance, music, socializing, and audiovisual experiences.

CCARC had not customarily purchased property up until that time. They either rented, or, better yet, found someone to donate the space they needed. The idea of going out on a financial limb with a significant real estate purchase was a frightening prospect. Lloyd George, one of those who personally pledged the first mortgage, recalled, "A number of us signed the note, but fortunately we never had to come up with any payments." Buying, using and reselling property became a hallmark of the Johnson regime. As a need arose, Johnson bought; as the organization outgrew the real estate, he sold, and bought a larger property.

Since Las Vegas property values were steadily increasing at the time, CCARC had gained another funding apparatus.

Johnson also announced another new plan that would become a foundation of Opportunity Village for the future. "We hope to eventually handle jobs for individual firms using assembly line type production," he said. "Possibilities could be mailing and packaging materials, wrapping candy bars, sorting generator parts, or assembling ball point pens."

The organization opened a thrift store on one of the stores on the South Main property, and today, with most vocational training taking place at the West Oakey and Henderson campuses, the entire South Main acreage is used for a giant thrift store with vocational training in a retail sales environment. Adults with intellectual disabilities are most comfortable in familiar surroundings; they do not adjust well to change. Thus, many of those Opportunity Village clients who work today in the South Main Street thrift store have been there since its inception. "The old trainees," Joylin Vanderberg called them; "still, they love that place . . . they love it!"

The South Main Street center also planned to conduct daily workshops to teach cooking, food preparation, serving skills and after meal cleanup with an eye toward future entry into the job market. Again, this modest beginning led to today's gleaming, state of the art kitchen at the West Oakey campus where a program for preparing high school students with intellectual disabilities for the workplace is combined with regular vocational training.

The center thus became partially self-supporting, with the remainder of the expenses covered by donations put into dozens of wishing wells CCARC had set up throughout the community. The group also purchased two apartment buildings on South Third Street for use as residence halls, the down payment

Variety School Graduates Six Students

GRADUATION—Variety School graduates, left to right, Claire Conant, Claudia Bailey, and Ann Clements, and Edward Kile. On the left, Howard J. Marr, principal; on the right, Charles Howell of the Variety Club.

65

★ ★ ★   ★ ★ ★   ★ ★ ★

The Variety School for Special Education recently held their annual "potluck" dinner and graduation ceremonies on the lawn adjacent to the school for the handicapped children. Approximately 200 parents and friends attended the ceremonies, at which time 6 students, age 18, received certificates of completion, presented by Howard J. Marr, principal.

An additional part of the ceremony included installation of P-TA officers for the 1965-66 school year and the presentation of personal gifts to the graduates by Charles Howell, representative of Variety Club.

A 1965 Las Vegas Review-Journal article honors Variety School graduates. Included were Claudia Bailey, now deceased, and Ann Clements, who still works at the downtown Thrift Store.

being donated by board member Walt Epprecht.

In 1972, Clark County Association of Retarded Children was renamed Opportunity Village Association for Retarded Citizens (OVARC) at the suggestion of Dr. Johnson. Its vocational training programs were making great strides: "With careful training, one boy is now able to hold down a job in a car wash and makes $350 a month," Dr. Robert Foster, the principal of the Helen J. Stewart School proudly told the *Las Vegas Review-Journal* in 1970. "Instead of being a burden on society, he is contributing to the economy, buying clothes and food, paying taxes. Another youth is wrapping potatoes in foil at a produce house, which prepares vegetables for the Strip hotels," Foster added.

The following year the original Opportunity Center on south Fourth Street was closed. By this time the facility was being used mainly to provide educational assistance to youngsters; but new legislation had mandated that task to the school system. The few adults that remained in the facility were absorbed into the Employment Training Center on south Main.

♥ ♥ ♥

The year 1975 was a landmark year for children with disabilities throughout the nation. Congress passed Public Law 94-142, the Education of All Handicapped Children Act, federal funds were made available, and states were mandated to develop and

A young Tommy Wilcox (kneeling) and another client assist Helen Dial with a tree trimming job at the first Opportunity Center in this early 1960s snapshot.

implement policies that assured a free, appropriate public education to all children with disabilities. Soon thereafter, the Opportunity Center on South Main transferred most of its vocational training to the West Oakey campus, where it remains today.

By the late 1970s, an activity center was added to house and train people with more severe disabilities unable to participate in the regular workshop program. Later called the Pre-Vocational Center, the goal was to train these people for eventual entrance into the more advanced vocational workshops.

A recycling yard and a gas station were also in operation, and a button and badge factory, the Nevada Badge Company, was opened. The badge company's operation was typical of the new directions in which Ted Johnson had led the organization. Workers were now called "employees," and were paid a wage for their efforts. The badge company was the only business of its type in southern Nevada, and made buttons and badges for politicians, entertainers and businesses. Included in the operation were a printing shop, a sewing operation that repaired industrial uniforms, and a department that installed velvet linings in jewelers' ring boxes. "How many buttons a person turns out isn't that important," a supervisor told the *Las Vegas Review-Journal* in 1977. "The main thing we're interested in is teaching people to come to work every day and to interact with a supervisor . . . skills necessary in terms of where we're going to place them in community jobs later."

Employees were identified by badges they could earn for the efficiency of their work. As each employee's work improved, he earned a higher level badge, which entitled him to a Coke® or other treat. There were also tokens earned for good behavior that could be used to purchase treats. Again, competition was only to improve one's own badge level, never to compete with other employees.

The procedures pioneered in the Nevada Badge Company were so successful that they were adopted for use by the thrift store, and eventually in all Opportunity Village's business and training facilities.

Success stories began making the rounds in the growing Las Vegas community, telling of men and women who had been taken off the public dole and were now leading useful,

fulfilled lives. One such case was thirty-two year old Frances Nast, blind and severely disabled.

"After thirty years of no help, and nowhere to turn," her mother said, "I found Opportunity Village. "We tried taking her there at first, but her behavior made it impossible," she related. Nast hadn't been out of the house for many years, and screamed at the top of her voice at strangers.

Opportunity Village buttons down order

By Ed Vogel
Review-Journal

The biggest Las Vegas boosters of Ronald Reagan this week are the people who work at Opportunity Village.

Employees are working overtime to finish making 250,000 buttons for the Reagan-Bush presidential campaign.

"By the time they are done, they will be sick of Reagan," quipped Opportunity Village Executive Director Jerry Allen.

The 250,000-button order is the largest ever handled by Opportunity Village.

More than 40 intellectually handicapped people are working evenings and weekends to complete the order in time for Reagan's upcoming campaign visits.

If Reagan goes to Florida, the buttons must arrive ahead of his visit. If he campaigns in Texas, then the buttons must be waiting for him there.

The order was offered to Opportunity Village by Sig Rogich, the Las Vegas advertising agency head who [is] busy this summer coordi[nating ad]vertising for the Reagan re-

Quotable

❛Normally an order like this would take us three weeks. This one we must finish in a week.❜

— **Jerry Allen**

election campaign.

Rogich, who serves on Opportunity Village's advisory board, asked [Al]len last Thursday if his people co[uld] handle the massive button ord[er.] Within a day, Allen formally place[d a] bid for the order and began order[ing] additional parts.

"Normally an order like this wo[uld] take us three weeks," he said. "T[his] one we must finish in a week."

Button-making is one of the [many] Opportunity Village industries. [The] agency makes 100,000 "I Love Ne[va]da" buttons a year. It also manufac[tures] buttons for most local polit[ical] candidates.

A small order of less than 100 b[uttons]
Please see BUTTONS,

Opportunity Village assigned a caseworker and a university psychology graduate student to help Nast. They visited her home daily for months to help her overcome her anger, fear and inappropriate behavior. Finally they began to see signs that their work was paying off. After many more months of work, Nast evolved into a happy, well adjusted person who learned to spend her days joyfully with friends at Opportunity Village. Too disabled to ever enter vocational training, still Nast's turnaround gave new meaning to her life, and some desperately needed respite for her family.

Dr. Ted Johnson left the organization he had served and nurtured for so many years in 1974 to return east. His tenure was only seven years, not long enough in the minds of most, but the direction he had

Gary Thompson/Review-Journal

Two clients in the button shop, John Riccobene (left) and Doug George, manufacture buttons in 1984 for the Reagan-Bush re-election campaign.

TONS FOR THE GIPPER - Opportunity Village workers John Riccobene, left, and Doug George rapidly manufacture buttons for the Reagan-Bush re-election campaign.

established for Opportunity Village during his time in Las Vegas set a standard that few could have met. He was truly, "the right man at the right time."

Johnson was followed as executive director by Fred Tenney, then two years later Thomas Groome assumed the post. On January 29, 1979, in the showroom of the Hacienda Hotel on the famed Las Vegas Strip, Opportunity Village celebrated its twenty-fifth anniversary at a special awards dinner. An article in the *Las Vegas Sun* summed up some of the organization's most noteworthy achievements during its first quarter-century:

> In its first 25 years of service, Opportunity Village has grown from a small grade school for mentally retarded to the highest quality, most comprehensive vocational training center for adults offered in the State of Nevada.

> "Credit for Opportunity Village's success must be given to its founders who had the vision and foresite [sic] to plan for the future, laying the foundation for special education and creating public awareness of the needs and abilities of the mentally retarded," said Tom Groome, executive director of Opportunity Village. "A total of 208 clients were enrolled in the Sheltered Workshop in 1978, with the average caseload being 150, and 33 clients were placed in jobs in the community . . . "

> "Opportunity Village . . . can look with pride at its past achievements and ahead with confidence in future challenges," said Groome.

♥ ♥ ♥

Dr. Ted Johnson, during his stay in Las Vegas, set Opportunity Village upon the course it would follow to the present day. He transitioned the organization from its service to children with mental retardation

to adults. Perhaps more importantly, Johnson seemed to be prescient in his belief that to depend solely upon government support would be a fool's mission. He realized that Opportunity Village had to be more than just a place where intellectually challenged adults could socialize and train for the workplace. To pay for all the services that would be necessary, he knew the organization also had to be a viable business that could earn its own money to support its many and varied programs.

It's doubtful even Johnson realized how well generations of management would succeed in building on the foundations he laid down. Today, Opportunity Village is still a place where adults with intellectual disabilities can develop social lives and train for the workplace. But it's also a successful thrift store, and a full service mailing house; a profitable button factory, and Southern Nevada's second largest document shredding company; an assembly and packaging business, and a huge custodial service provider; a food service giant, and the most successful special events producer in a city famous for such things.

But it almost didn't turn out that way.

By late 1988, two decades had passed since the organization had obtained its two-and-a-half acre parcel of land from the BLM. The State of Nevada had by now built three mental health facilities on its share of the Charleston property, while Opportunity Village continued to make-do at their increasingly dilapidated work center facility. But finally, the leaky roof, overcrowded conditions, and growing client base had convinced the organization that it was time to move forward with new facilities.

Remembering all the promises they had been given over the intervening years for additional space if they needed it, Opportunity Village requested a ten acre parcel for a planned five building complex on the mental health center's eighty acres. It was then, however,

Opportunity Village clients enjoy an outing to Nellis Air force Base in the 1970s.

that the organization got a lesson in the vicissitudes of political promises.

"Sorry, we don't have any space for you," the state government told Opportunity Village. They explained that the three existing facilities had already used up half of the eighty acres, and all three had expansion plans. On top of that, a new facility for the criminally insane was to be added to the grounds, leaving no space available for any "private" use.

The "enemy" within the state was soon identified. It was Marvin Sedway, a Las Vegas assemblyman who was chairman of the powerful Ways and Means Committee, the state government body in charge of doling out funding for such projects.

"We need that land," Sedway said, explaining the need in a none too sensitive manner when he added, "We have a lot of crazies running around in Las Vegas." He proceeded to instruct the state human resources director to develop a master plan for the acreage that would exclude Opportunity Village and any other private organization.

Sedway's words, and his attitude, set off a fire storm of protest in Southern Nevada. "Without Opportunity Village's assistance the state may never had obtained the land . . ." an editorial in the *Las Vegas Sun* decried. A 1968 letter from the then manager of the state planning board was uncovered and published in the newspapers, backing up the organization's claims.

As a concession, Opportunity Village offered to give up its two-and-a-half acre parcel in return for the right to lease the needed ten acres. They would relocate their planned retail processing center and thrift store to another site, they said.

Instead of relenting in the face of the group's concession, Assemblyman Sedway turned up the heat. He ordered an appraisal on Opportunity Village's two-and-a-half acres, and announced that the State was going to buy it, by eminent domain if necessary, denying them even the small parcel they already held a deed for. It was at this point that even the mere survival of Opportunity Village became questionable.

Petitions signed by hundreds of Southern Nevada business and civic leaders were sent to the office of Governor Bob Miller requesting his intervention. He had initially backed Sedway's stubborn refusal to bend on the issue, but by this time, he was beginning to sense the political folly of his stand. He agreed to meet with a delegation from Southern Nevada, composed of popular ex-governor and *Las Vegas Sun* editor Mike O'Callaghan, and influential advertising executive and Republican power broker Sig Rogich.

Following the meeting, there was talk of compromise, and the following week details began to emerge. The fifty-bed hospital for the criminally insane would be located not in the mental health complex but atop the downtown Clark County Detention Facility. For their part, Opportunity Village officials agreed to give up their small parcel and in return receive a long term, low cost lease on six acres of property within the complex.

In the wake of the compromise, Assemblyman Sedway told the *Las Vegas Sun*, "I did take a strong approach to this, but I was persuaded I was wrong."

Asked by whom, he replied with a smile, "By the Governor and his staff, who showed me the error of my ways."

"I did take a strong approach to this, but I was persuaded I was wrong."
— Marvin Sedway

"That was a turning point for Opportunity Village, a watershed event," chief development officer Linda Smith said. Never again has the organization been willing to settle for whatever crumbs federal, state or local government may try to pass off on it. From that day forward, Opportunity Village's clients would either be treated justly, or there would be hell to pay.

It was a rewarding victory indeed.

♥ ♥ ♥

Before ending the story of the founding and early years of Opportunity Village, it is necessary to finish the story of the family that launched it all, the Baileys.

Claudia Bailey began her education at the Updike School after her mother's heroic fight, and eventually graduated from the Variety School in 1965 at eighteen years of age. After graduation, she immediately became part of Opportunity Village's adult program.

A 1974 article in the *Las Vegas Review-Journal* described Claudia's life at Opportunity Village:

She has learned to assist in the kitchen, making salads, preparing other foods, and other kitchen duties. She enjoys dancing, TV, and is part of the family picture in whatever is planned. Like all young ladies she is concerned with retaining a very lovely figure and is quiet diet conscious. When her brother married, Claudia was the flower girl and vied with the bride for bouquets of admiration. She is petite, with short fashionably dressed dark hair, beautiful complexion and a heart stopping smile.

Meanwhile, Patrick "Pat" Bailey married Danna Lynn Crist of Bremerton, Washington, in 1966, following college and a four-year stint in the United States Navy. After living in Las Vegas for a year the couple relocated to Danna's hometown of Bremerton, where they still reside.

Pat was a huge help in telling this story. Without his personal recollections and reminiscences, the story of the early years of Opportunity Village and his parents' fight for Claudia would not have been possible.

Elbert "Al" Bailey retired from the Union Pacific Railroad in 1976. An avid fisherman and a terrific engine mechanic, he spent his retirement years working on his boat and taking the family on regular boating and fishing trips to Lake Mead. Along with Dessie, he continued to work with Opportunity Village where Claudia remained as a happy client.

In the early 1990s Bailey began showing signs of dementia. Eventually, when he no longer even recognized family members, he was put into an Alzheimer's facility in Henderson. Al Bailey died of pneumonia on December 30, 1993, two months shy of his eightieth birthday.

If this story has a genuine hero, it is Dessie Bailey. She continued to be somewhat involved with Opportunity Village the entire time Claudia was a client at the facility, but at a greatly reduced level. In 1996 she began showing the same signs of Alzheimer's disease that had claimed her husband Al. As she was alone, son Pat and his wife Danna moved her to a convalescent home in Bremerton to be close to them.

Claudia continued at Opportunity Village, but lived with a caretaker in Henderson once her mother was no longer able to care for her at home. At about the same time as her mother moved to Bremerton, Claudia's caregiver was forced to give up her responsibility. Pat and Danna Bailey moved Claudia to a home near Bremerton, in Port Orchard, Washington.

Dessie Lola Bailey died on November 28, 1999, at eighty-one-years old. Just over a year later, on December 12, 2000, Claudia Bailey passed away from pneumonia at fifty-three.

It's time for us to shift gears a bit as we look back — and forward — at Opportunity Village. These first five chapters have looked at Opportunity Village from the outside in; the next seven chapters will be looking from the inside out. We're going to take an internal look at the people, the places, and the programs that have made this organization truly a one of a kind phenomenon; the community that claims it as "Las Vegas favorite charity;" and the future for this unique organization, the clients it serves, and the community that loves and supports it.

Artwork by client, Clarissa.

CHAPTER SIX

Staff & Volunteers:
Angels Among Us

*Oh, I believe there are angels among us
Sent down to us from somewhere up above.
They come to you and me in our darkest hours
To show us how to live, to teach us how to give,
To guide us with a light of love.*

— *Chorus from "Angels Among Us" by Becky Hobbs*

The words to this country song, written by country singing star Becky Hobbs, and recorded by the group Alabama, stayed on the Billboard Top Singles chart for over a year. You'll also find the title phrase used on everything from printed prayers to coffee mugs, perhaps because it resonates in so many different ways with so many different people. It certainly resonates with the hundreds of clients at Opportunity Village whose lives have been so enriched by the men and women who have forsaken other, more lucrative careers to follow their hearts and serve their fellow man.

♥ ♥ ♥

Ed Guthrie, the Executive Director of Opportunity Village for the past thirteen years, grew up like most other young people of the turbulent 1960s. Referring to his two years at the University of Maryland in the late 1960s, near his hometown of Washington D. C., he said, "I majored in partying and opposing the war in Vietnam." When a flash of realism finally struck him, he decided he should drop out of the school before they kicked him out, "because I realized I might want to go back some day."

Like many others in the idealistic but adventure-some early boomer generation, Guthrie spent the next few years working at odd jobs and traveling the world. "I would work like a dog, save my money, and travel. Then work like a dog again, save my money, and travel," he remembered.

After a few years of the vagabond life, Guthrie arranged to meet a friend who owed him some money at Mardi Gras in New Orleans. The money arrived, the friend did not, but Guthrie partied on without him. As chance would have it, he met a young lady of equally free spirit, and six months later they were married.

Like Ed, his new wife Sheryl had dropped out of college, so they both enrolled at tiny St. Mary's

Ed Guthrie admires the collating work being done by Tracy Peterson in the employment training center.

College of Maryland to finish their education. "We were as poor as church mice," he recalled, so when they discovered a summer internship program offered at the college that paid cash, room and board, they couldn't resist. The program involved working with people with intellectual disabilities in one of the nation's earliest deinstitutionalized programs. Both of the young people immediately fell in love with the work, changed their college majors, and graduated two years later with degrees in social work.

Eventually the couple ended up in Rochester, New York, where Guthrie was the director of a small program for people with mental retardation. "When I started with the agency our budget was $120,000 a year, and $12,000 of it was me," he said. He spent the next fifteen years building the program, adding services, and expanding the agency's reach to serve a wider range of intellectually and physically disabled people. But when the governing board decided to stop growing the agency, Guthrie knew it was time to move on.

A friend recommended him to Opportunity Village, and although he and Sheryl wanted to remain in the East, when an offer came, they accepted. That was 1994, and Guthrie said his goal for Opportunity Village has never changed. "We're a community rehabilitation program," he said. "Our aim is to get people back into the community — or into the community in the first place — so they can have jobs and a place to fit in."

"The only way to train people to work is to have them working, and to do that we have to be a good business. So we have to balance those two things, the mission and the money, to be successful," he said.

Under Ed Guthrie's direction, and with the help and support of an excellent staff, Opportunity Village has been successfully balancing the mission and the money ever since. Guthrie emphasized the importance of the staff in that balancing act: "They're here because they have a passion for what they do and a passion for the people we serve. That makes being the boss lots easier, because they're here because they want to be here."

"Do we agree all the time?" he asked. "No, but at least everybody's heart is in the right place; everybody means well."

Looking to the future, Guthrie sees the biggest challenge as managing growth. "The community has had a problem developing the social infrastructure that goes with the explosive population growth we've experienced," Guthrie said.

"The physical infrastructure — the pipes and the roads and such — we seem to be well aware of that, and we're aware of the educational infrastructure too . . . building new schools, hiring new teachers. But I'm not sure we're aware of the social infrastructure that has to grow at the same time."

Guthrie pointed out that of the 5,000 to 7,000 people who move into Las Vegas every month, fifty to seventy will need the services of an organization like Opportunity Village. "I don't know anywhere else in the country where they have to learn how to serve that many new people every month," he said. Opportunity Village could make the decision simply not to grow, but that would be a disservice to all the

> *"Do we agree all the time? . . . No, but at least everybody's heart is in the right place; everybody means well."*

people who need the services, or will need the services in the future.

♥ ♥ ♥

"Nonprofit workers come in two varieties, paid and unpaid," according to a 1998 book on nonprofit compensation practices, written by Carol Barbeito and Jack Bowman. Although the statistics in the book would be too dated to provide any meaningful information in this day and age, most of the basic tenets remain unchanged.

"In a typical nonprofit organization, the volunteer board of directors is a group of unpaid workers that carry out the governing role," the book continues. "They hire a paid executive director to recruit and organize the rest of the workforce. The paid staff,

both at the executive and at other levels, recruits and works to motivate and retain volunteers."

Opportunity Village operates in much the same way as this typical nonprofit company described by the authors. There is one significant difference, however, a result of the size and complexity of Opportunity Village versus the typical nonprofit.

Opportunity Village is actually two separate corporations, the two being commonly referred to as the ARC side and the foundation side. The ARC side is the operations departments, while the foundation side is the fundraising and grants departments. Each corporation is governed by a separate volunteer board of directors, thus Opportunity Village is governed by two different boards. While not important to

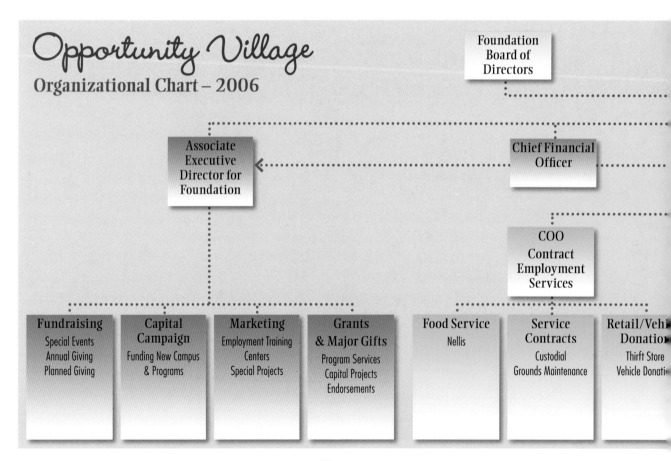

Opportunity Village

Organizational Chart – 2006

Foundation Board of Directors

Associate Executive Director for Foundation

Chief Financial Officer

COO Contract Employment Services

Fundraising	Capital Campaign	Marketing	Grants & Major Gifts	Food Service	Service Contracts	Retail/Vehi Donatio
Special Events Annual Giving Planned Giving	Funding New Campus & Programs	Employment Training Centers Special Projects	Program Services Capital Projects Endorsements	Nellis	Custodial Grounds Maintenance	Thrift Store Vehicle Donati

the thrust of this story, this does explain the organizational chart you see. Ed Guthrie, as executive director, answers to both boards; and two associate executive directors head the two separate corporations, under Guthrie's leadership.

A few years ago, Ed Guthrie and the two boards of directors saw the handwriting on the wall: Opportunity Village was going to have to restructure the organization in order to compete more effectively for work contracts with the for-profit sector. A stroll through one of the two employment training centers, where assembly and collating contracts were being fulfilled, was all any businessman needed to see to know that changes had to be made. Dozens of clients — the name used for those people with a disability who work at Opportunity Village — sat at the worktables chatting idly with one another. Here and there a client even had his or her head down on the table, taking a nap. Supervisors were constantly hurrying toward the door, looking for people who will habitually leave the room and roam the premises if they have no work to do.

Even those who were working were doing so in a desultory fashion. Some were slowly screwing a nut onto a bolt, then taking it back off and starting over. Others would string a few beads on a wire, then take them off, and repeat the process over and over. Sales and marketing manager Laura D'Amore, who was the general manager of the employment training centers at the time,

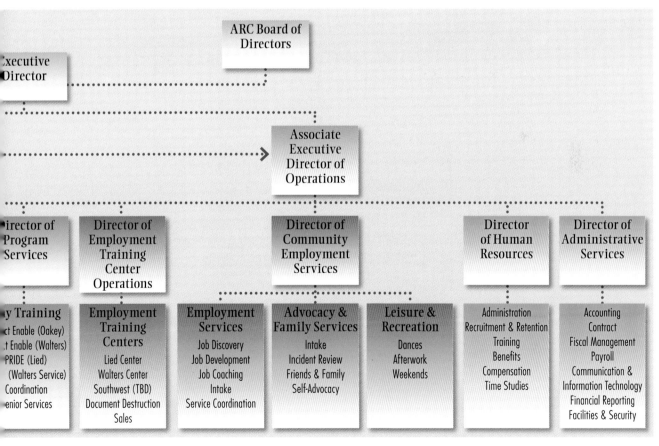

Jean Perry shares a light moment with Ed Guthrie.

said with a grin, "We were enhancing their fine motor skills."

It's funny today, but D'Amore said there was nothing funny about it back then. "Work came in sporadically," she said, "and we had to find something to keep people busy." The employment training center had a very large, ongoing contract with a national airline to replace the spongy ear plugs on their in-flight headsets, but after 9/11, and the cessation of most air travel, the contract dried up, and eventually disappeared altogether when the airline went into bankruptcy.

It was then that Ed Guthrie and the two boards realized that a new world was dawning, and that Opportunity Village had to change in order to compete. What has emerged is a new business attitude that is replacing the not-for-profit attitude that has prevailed since the organization's founding. With so many new people with disabilities entering the programs, there is a realization that in order to offer training and employment to all these people, Opportunity Village must be ready, willing and able to compete for work contracts with the for-profit sector. It is no longer possible, as it was for many years, to secure work by simply asking businesses to "hire the handicapped." That mantra is dead. It is now necessary to offer services whose price and quality is on a par with — or superior to — those offered by private industry.

The first move in this fundamental philosophical shift was to hire Jean Perry, a twenty-five-year veteran of health care industry management. Perry was named Associate Executive Director, and put in charge of the entire operations side of the organization. Contract employment services, the department that oversees all outside service contract work, and employment training center operations, the department that oversees all vocational training, had always been under one director. The two were separated, each with its own director, Kurt Weinrich and Mac Seabald. Both men came from the for-profit sector, Weinrich from the food and beverage side of the hotel/casino industry and Seabald from manufacturing. Each man brought a new business orientation to Opportunity Village, and each one has been toiling ever since to change the not-for-profit mentality of the people and programs under his jurisdiction.

The sales function, to secure contracts to employ clients during their vocational training, had always been part of the foundation side of the organization, where all fundraising, special events, and marketing activity resided. In the restructuring, that function was moved over to the operations side. Sales manager Laura D'Amore now works directly with Mac Seabald and the remainder of the vocational training department.

Jean Perry sees all the restructuring as a vital part of Opportunity Village's plan for the future.

Perry is a native of Long Island, New York, and began her health care career as a registered nurse. She is quick to admit, however, that her first love has always been to serve in a community-based health environment, so after only a brief stint as a hospital nurse, she moved to a home health organization, then into a management role. After acquiring a master's degree in health care administration, she immersed herself in the home and community health care industry.

In 1991 Perry and her family moved to Las Vegas where she ran Sierra Health Services' home health agency. After about twelve years of starting and managing a number of new programs and facilities for Sierra, Perry became vice president of operations for the Culinary Workers Union Health and Welfare Fund. In mid-2005 she was recruited to join Opportunity Village and set it on its future course.

"Change was difficult," she admitted. "The organization had always operated on a day-to-day basis; but we realized we had to build a solid foundation that would serve us well into the future . . . without losing the personal touch."

"We talk-the-talk and we walk-the-walk here . . . we truly are about the individuals we serve," Perry said proudly. "There's no ego or personal goals on the table; this is about the people we serve."

With the organizational restructuring mostly behind them, Perry said, Opportunity Village is now working toward maximizing their revenue streams so they can fund not only the existing programs but also all the new programs that are on the horizon. These new programs will be discussed more fully in chapter thirteen.

♥ ♥ ♥

Staffing a large not-for-profit organization like Opportunity Village is not a simple task. Over and above normal staffing problems faced by private sector employers, today's not-for-profit is often governed by a tangle of federal, state, and occasionally local laws and regulations. Charged with understanding and abiding by all these regulations is Kathy Ferguson, Opportunity Village's director of human resources.

A four-year employee herself, Ferguson came to the organization with more than twenty-five-years of human resources experience, mostly in banking and health management.

The simplest way to understand Opportunity Village's diverse workforce is to think of it as five separate groups of people. The first three groups are all considered employees of Opportunity Village, and they receive pay and benefits from the company just as they would from any for-profit employer. The fourth group is composed of clients who are engaged in vocational training. They are not considered employees, although most of them are paid a wage for the work they accomplish while undergoing their training. The clients in this group do not receive any company benefits.

The fifth group is composed of volunteers. Obviously they are not employees, and receive no pay or benefits for their work. Make no mistake, however, their contributions are vital to the success of the company.

Let's take a look at each group separately. Group one is composed of regular staff personnel, people in administration, fund raising, marketing, supervisory roles, and those who work directly with Opportunity Village's clients. As of early 2006, there were 236 people employed in these positions.

Group two is composed of clients. These clients work in the community at large on an Opportunity Village administered work service contract. These contracts are with federal, state, or local governments, or with private industry. Most, but not all, are for custodial or food service help, and these men and women earn a per-hour wage for their work. On federal contracts, a minimum pay rate is mandated; on all other contracts, Opportunity Village's pay rates are negotiated with the customer based upon prevailing local pay scales.

Much more will be said about these clients in group two, and the vocational training they receive in order to be work-qualified, in chapter seven. As of early 2006, there were nearly 150 people employed in this group.

Group three employees are also mostly custodial and food service people. They are men and women who are hired to either back-fill the work contracts when there are not enough clinets trained or available at any given time. This is the trickiest and most difficult group to administer from a human resources point of view, for a number of reasons. First, due to the burgeoning hospitality industry in Las Vegas, competition for workers is intense, and not-for-profit wage scales often lag private industry scales for this unskilled or semi-skilled labor. Second, federal work contracts mandate that the jobs must go to people with disabilities when they are available and trained to work. Thus, it is often necessary to juggle the employees, moving them from one job to another, as employees with disabilities come on line. These two factors increase turnover among these group three employees, often making the openings difficult to fill.

As of early 2006, there were thirty of these group three employees on the Opportunity Village payroll.

Pay scales for non-disabled employees, those in groups one and three, are based upon wages for comparable work in the private sector. Generally, but not always, Opportunity Village's scales lag private industry scales somewhat. However, this disparity is often overcome through a very generous benefits package. In an era when private industry benefit packages are in full retreat, Opportunity Village benefits are actually increasing.

Each employee in groups one and three is entitled to a medical/dental plan that is eighty percent company paid. For eligible family members, this plan is fifty percent paid by the company. A vision plan is 100 percent paid by the company. Both long-term and short-term disability plans, and a paid time-off program are also in place. Employees also receive a retirement savings plan where the company offers a fifty cents match for each dollar saved by the employee, to a limit of $4,000 annually of his deferrals.

In their book on nonprofit compensation, Carol L. Barbeito and Jack P. Bowman state that many nonprofits include innovative ideas in their benefits packages to attract and keep good employees. Opportunity Village has such an innovative benefit. Every employee is eligible to receive a $10,000 loan to purchase a home. Each year, twenty percent of the loan is excused, so that after five years of employment the loan becomes an outright gift. A number of employees have taken advantage of the benefit so far, and Ferguson believes the number will grow.

Finally, these employees are offered extensive educational and training opportunities at no cost. This training normally exceeds the training necessary for a person to learn his own job, and thus positions him for a better job within the company, or in another company should he elect to leave.

Many of the courses are offered by NISH, the national organization that creates employment opportunities for people with severe disabilities. A few examples are: "Problem Solving and Decision Making," "Improving People, Performance and Results," and "Art of Negotiation." There is also a roster of courses that serve specific vocational areas in which Opportunity Village operates: "How to Run a Custodial Services Project" and "How to Run a Food Service Project," to name but a couple. For those who desire a career in social work, or in developmental disability work, the training is priceless, and can lead to a college level associates, bachelors or masters degree.

. . . each succeeding generation has produced its fair share of these unselfish men and women, these "angels among us."

"Many of our hires are people who may not otherwise have the opportunity to get such specialized training," Human Resources Director Ferguson pointed out. "We're offering these people a hand up, just as we offer one to the people we serve, our clients."

There are a number of appeals Opportunity Village relies on to attract good people. Benefits and training are two of the major ones. But another, less obvious benefit is the mission itself. There exists in the workforce men and women who simply want to work in an environment where they can contribute to their fellow man. They honestly and genuinely want to give something back. These are the same kind of people who began flocking to the Peace Corps in 1961, and each succeeding generation has produced its fair share of these unselfish men and women, these "angels among us." Ferguson relates to these people; it was the same calling that enticed her to leave private industry and join Opportunity Village.

Today, especially designed personality profile tests and other screening techniques are used to single out these people from among the many applicants, and it's one of the joys of the job when a match is made.

Ferguson takes pride in the fact that turnover among non-disabled employees is at an annual rate of only thirty-eight percent, unusually low for service sector jobs. That compares to an annual turnover rate of forty-five percent for the companies Opportunity Village competes most closely with for employees, and a rate of ninety-nine percent for the service sector in the Las Vegas metro area as a whole.

Pay and benefits for the clients, those who work in our group two on a service contract, are quite different. The pay rate each worker earns is established by a rather complex formula. It begins with average pay rates within the community for each type of job, and is then factored downward based upon time studies of how much work the person is able to perform versus his non-disabled fellow worker. If the work performance of the two is equal, the pay rate is equal; if the worker performs at twenty-five percent lower productivity, his pay is twenty-five percent less.

These disabled workers are eligible for the regular staff benefits package discussed above if they work under one of Opportunity Village's state, local or private service contracts. If they work under a federal contract, their benefits are different, as mandated by law. In that case they receive a health and welfare cash benefit from Opportunity Village that they can use to pay for their medical and/or dental care, or apply toward retirement, at their option.

All disabled citizens also receive special Social Security benefits, and qualify for certain Medicare or Medicaid benefits as well. However, this government support is rarely enough to cover the myriad of expenses that go with these disabilities. Thus, the income the clients can earn, whether from a work service contract, an independent job in the community, or as a part of an vocational training program, is an important issue for the client and his or her caregiver.

Occasionally, individuals who entered Opportunity Village as clients are able to work their way up to a regular staff position. It was discovered that one client, a young man, had unusually sound skills with a computer. Today, he is an administrative support staffer.

This is not the only such situation. Other men and women with mild disabilities now fill regular staff positions in supervisory roles on both federal and local work contracts, a point of real pride for the entire organization. The story of one such young man, Nehemiah Gipson, is told in chapter eight.

Linda Smith has enjoyed a career spanning more than three decades with the organization. She began as a volunteer in 1970. Her husband at that time, Glenn Smith, whose story is told in chapter ten, was working an entertainment gig in Las Vegas, and Linda had accompanied him. To fill her days while Glenn was practicing, she began volunteering at the Opportunity Village thrift store. She was pregnant at the time with son Chris, who in 1971 was born with Down syndrome, so Linda Smith's volunteer choice seems prophetic as you look back on it. In 1976, the couple moved permanently to Las Vegas.

With Chris attending special education classes, Smith wanted to work. But she was a dancer, and the only available dancing jobs were topless. So she did a little convention modeling, and again volunteered at Opportunity Village.

In 1981, Opportunity Village dropped out of United Way because its policies restricted the group's independent fund raising plans. Smith was offered the job as their first full time fundraiser, and she accepted. Today, in addition to being one of two Associate Executive Directors under Executive Director Ed Guthrie, she also serves as Chief Development Officer. In the latter job, she oversees all marketing and community relations activities as well as fundraising, major capital campaigns, and grants. Not only is Smith known and loved by every client at Opportunity Village, she is also widely recognized as the "public face" of the fifty-three year old organization.

"I know I've made my mark here," Linda Smith admits. "As the public face of Opportunity Village for so many years, I'm like the Energizer® bunny out there. But I don't do it alone. We have such a great staff . . . we're all joined at the hip here; and I get very self-conscious about getting so much credit for what has been a total team effort."

One story in particular goes a long way toward explaining Smith's special understanding of and compassion for people with mental retardation and their families.

In the early 1970s, when the family still lived in Toronto, Glenn got a Christmas gig in New York. So they could spend the holidays together, the entire family decided to go with him for his appearance. At the border, Glenn and Linda presented their green cards. The U.S. border agent studied the documents, then pointed at the baby who was sitting quietly in the back seat and asked for his documents, something that had never happened before. The couple admitted he had none.

The border agent studied Chris closely, noticing the just-emerging signs of Down syndrome, slightly slanting eyes and lack of physical coordination. He asked the family to accompany him into his office, where the Smiths informed him their son was intellectually disabled. Any attempt at understanding or compassion immediately drained out of the man, and he began thumbing quickly through his manual.

"Here it is," he announced triumphantly. "Section 212-A of the Immigration Act states clearly that he's not welcome in this country without a special visa." Three-year old Chris, they were informed, was classified as an "undesirable alien." According to Linda, American immigration law at the time placed Chris just barely above criminals as the least desirable people to be admitted to the U.S.

Despite desperate pleadings to allow the family to spend Christmas together, the border agent was adamant. He would not even allow the mother and her baby to wait in his office while Glenn's brother

Linda Smith checks out one of the Magical Forest permanent displays.

drove one hundred miles from Toronto to pick them up, while Glenn proceeded on to his engagement in New York.

In a 1987 newspaper article, Smith told how she and Glenn would come to realize how blessed they had been with Chris. "He always brings out the very best in us," she said. "He brought out in me compassion that I never knew I had, and he taught us humility. I think we needed him more than he needed us," she admitted.

That same compassion and humility have served Smith well in her present role. When she first joined the staff as a fundraiser, she said she was scared to death; "I didn't think I was capable of handling it," she said. But handle it she did, rising through the ranks to become one of the most respected women in Nevada today. She and Glenn were divorced some years ago, and today she is remarried to one of Opportunity Village's advisory board members and most generous benefactors, John Wasserburger, although she still retains the name Smith in her professional role.

Like all parents of a child with an intellectual disability, despite their age, Smith worries about what could happen to Chris when she dies. Chris's disability is such that he will never be able to achieve a higher functioning level. So where could he go, if another family member could not take him in?

"In Las Vegas, there is a real shortage of housing for people with intellectual disabilities," Smith said. "Group homes have a waiting list; and even when a place does become available, it may not be a good fit." She admits that Chris is probably safe, because there is family and financial resources. But for many lower income families, and those without an extended family, the problem is very real. In those cases, the person with this disability becomes a ward of the state, and is placed in a state residential facility.

Group homes are the best alternative, but Nevada lags behind other states in allocating funds to support such facilities. Chapter thirteen discusses Opportunity Village's hope to become involved in providing housing at some future time.

❤ ❤ ❤

One of the chief factors in management's knack for keeping their payroll at a reasonable level over the years has been their innate ability to find and keep a wonderful staff of volunteers. Over the years, these men and women have numbered in the thousands, but one very special lady stands out.

Winifred "Winnie" Winters, now in her early eighties, has been volunteering her time and talents to the organization for nearly a quarter century. This isn't volunteer work for Winters, it's a job, even though a paycheck does not go along with it. Every Monday through Friday from 10 AM until 3:30 PM, you'll find Winters working at her desk in the resource development department, or bustling between buildings, at the campus on West Oakey.

Winters and her husband Ed, who is now deceased, came to Las Vegas in 1984 after he had retired from the phone company on Long Island. He had acquired training and a license to perform Swedish massage, and immediately found work. Winters wasted no time looking for her own "job" as a volunteer. It was November, and Opportunity Village had a gift wrapping booth at the Boulevard Mall, so she began wrapping Christmas presents that very day. When the holidays were over, Winters marched over to the training facility on Main Street and announced that she wanted to volunteer every day. "They gave me some little things to do," she said with a sparkle in her blue eyes," and they never told me not to come back. So I just kept going in."

Winnie Winters is still going in. A beautiful, trim lady (she still walks regularly) with curly silver hair piled on top of her head, she has a ready smile and a cheerful word for everyone. Asked what her duties are today, she said in typical self-deprecating fashion, "Oh, my duties are getting lighter and lighter . . . I just do piddling little things . . . but I can always find something to do."

As if to contradict that remark, a young man from another office walked in at just that moment and asked Winters if she could arrange to get 150 gift packages wrapped for a employment training center customer. Naturally, like all such jobs, it had to be completed in very short order. "Well, I guess so," she said, smiling at him.

For many years, Winters oversaw the gift wrap booth where she began working, and over the years the humble little kiosk raised $350,000 for the organization.

Since beginning at Opportunity Village, Winters has had a hand in almost every part of the organization at one time or another. And her generous work has not been confined to the office. In 2005, Winters was awarded a Daily Points of Light award from the Points of Light Foundation for her volunteerism, which said in part:

In addition to her many years of service, she has provided a home to people with intellectual dis-

"Winnie" Winters has volunteered at Opportunity Village for nearly a quarter century.

abilities who have no families to depend on. Ms. Winters feeds and clothes them, takes them to special events and introduces them to a concept of love that they may never have experienced.

A newspaper article in 2001 also related the story of another client Winters had taken under her wing. He loved Bingo, but couldn't read the cards. So Winters personally took him to adult literacy classes at the University of Nevada, Las Vegas until he could read.

Winters has also been honored with a national Lifelong Achievement Award by the Association of Retarded Citizens, and Opportunity Village has named her Volunteer of the Year. The group also surprised her with the "Ed and Winnie Winters Circle of Friends Garden" to reflect their love and respect for her. The little year-round garden next to the gymnasium brightens the day of every client and staffer who visits it.

Not bad recognitions for a person who only does "piddling little things."

The Points of Light Award sums up Winnie Winters perfectly: "Because of Ms. Winters, thousands of disabled people in Las Vegas know the improved financial and emotional quality of life that comes with active employment."

Amen to that.

In addition to Winnie Winters, there are about seventy volunteers who come in either regularly or on an as needed basis to assist the paid staff with office duties, working with clients, and various other responsibilities. This entire group of volunteers is known as "Winnie's crew." It is to this group too that Winters goes when she needs immediate assistance, such as wrapping the 150 gifts packages that found its way to her desk.

♥ ♥ ♥

Left: Nancy Leins, employment training center supervisor, assists Sheila Duckworth on the assembly line. Right: employment training center supervisor June Jones instructs Catherine Bonsangue in her work.

Among all the regular staff positions at Opportunity Village, according to insiders, none are as rewarding, or as challenging, as those that require constant face-to-face contact with the clients. Nancy Leins and June Jones certainly appreciate that fact better than anyone. Both ladies are employment training center supervisors, and spend their entire days working directly with the clients on assembly and collation contracts.

Jones, originally from Minnesota, began working for Opportunity Village in the mid 1980s when the employment training center was located on West Charleston Boulevard, next to the old Holsum Bakery. She spent ten years on the job, then left to become

a food service worker at Silverton Hotel/Casino for the next ten years. As if on cue, she began to miss the work at Opportunity Village, and especially all the clients who had become friends, so about four years ago, she left her better paying job and returned to the employment training center.

Jones has a grandson, twenty-seven-years old, who works with the clients in Project ENABLE who have more profound disabilities, a fact that lights up her face with pride as she relates it. She also has a son and daughter who live in Las Vegas.

Nancy Leins is from Memphis, Tennessee, and moved to Las Vegas in 1964. "I never had to work," she admitted with a wry smile; "I was a domestic engineer." But following a divorce, she attended a two week course sponsored by a Christian Society in Texas. Following the aptitude tests and evaluation, they told Leins she would be happiest in social work, helping other people. Although that came as a surprise to her, when she returned home she started her first job at Opportunity Village, also at the old West Charleston Employment Training Center.

Both ladies smiled at the recollection of the old building, which was called "Noah's Ark" due to its penchant for flooding during every heavy rain. They also fondly recalled the Holsum Bakery next door. It's now a converted collection of art galleries and chic urban lofts, but a quarter-century ago, the delicious aroma of baking bread often tantalized the clients to slip away and snatch hot loaves off the assembly line. "One client we couldn't find," Jones remembered with a laugh. "We finally found him in the bakery truck, just eating away at the bread."

Laughter quickly turned to tears when Leins was asked the main appeal of her job. "I feel so rewarded when my day is over," she said emotionally. "You just feel so good about yourself because you know you've done something . . . you've really helped people."

"When you're training somebody on a new job, and they *finally* get it, you feel great," Jones added. "When they've got it, you know they're going to make more money because they got it. It's just a great feeling."

Although each lady loves every client she works with, it's a moment of great satisfaction when one of their own is able to advance to a better job. But there are low points too, especially when a client is ill. Some have seizures; some have uncontrollable behavioral outbursts. These things are heartbreaking to all the staff.

Asked what qualities it takes to succeed in a position that demands so much of a person, both agreed patience and caring top the list. "You have to really want to do this," Leins said; "and you'll know in the first week if it's right for you."

Jones, as a grade-one supervisor, oversees six clients. Leins is a grade-two supervisor, and oversees sixteen of her own clients, and other supervisors and their clients as well, for a total of forty clients. In partially funding this training, the state mandates a certain ratio of supervisors to clients, which depends upon the functioning level of each client. The work of the supervisors isn't simply to oversee the clients; they are also responsible for the work product, and must see that production quotas are met.

It's not an easy job. It is a job that many people would not be able to handle. But for Nancy Leins and June Jones, there is no job they'd rather have. Leins lives in the tiny desert town of Alamo, about seventy-five miles north of Las Vegas, and she commutes three hours a day to work and home. Yet she refuses to complain. "What a privilege I've been given to help somebody else," she said.

Authors Barbeito and Bowman, in their book about nonprofit compensation, spoke about the importance of organizations like Opportunity Village, and the people who work there:

> Nonprofit organizations carry in them the heart of our society. They perform the functions that make us civilized: caring for the dying, teaching children, protecting the environment, and releasing beauty.
>
> Without them, it is hard to imagine what our world would be like.

*Project ENABLE staffer Rayfield Hearon
assists John Dorsey in learning a simple
three-into-one assembly project.*

CHAPTER SEVEN

Vocational Training:
I Can Do That!

Many things have changed since Thomas Wilcox entered Opportunity Village as one of its first adult clients. The process for having a person admitted to the group today is more complex, thanks mainly to the tangle of laws that now govern these services.

When a young man or woman with an intellectual disability is aged out of the Clark County School system on their twenty-second birthday, if they haven't left earlier, they become eligible to join Opportunity Village as a client, if space is available. Their parents or caregiver do not simply show up on the doorstep asking to have their son or daughter placed in vocational training. They must first apply to the Desert Regional Center (DRC,) the state agency through which government funds flow to partially pay for their vocational training.

Each person is assigned to a DRC caseworker where he is carefully tested and evaluated. The caseworker coordinates with an Opportunity Village intake service coordinator, and the two decide into which program the applicant should be placed, based upon his or her current capabilities. There is a hierarchical structure of the programs within Opportunity Village.

Those with the most profound physical and intellectual disabilities are placed in Project PRIDE. This program is for young men and women who require round-the-clock care and monitoring, and will probably never be able to participate in any type of vocational training.

Those with slightly higher abilities, but still very limited, are placed in Project ENABLE. Some of these low functioning individuals are able to perform basic collating functions, and are paid a stipend for their work at such a task. But most, like their colleagues in Project PRIDE, will never be able to participate in more advanced vocational training, or gain work in the community.

Next up the ladder are those who function at a higher level, and are placed in a vocational training program. These are Opportunity Village's Employment Centers. Here, working in large group settings, the clients perform basic packaging and assembly, sewing, button making and mass mailing jobs, for which they receive a regular paycheck. Those who work in the organization's thrift store and document destruction business are also part of this group.

These clients are not considered employees of Opportunity Village; they are part of the vocational training program, and may or may not ever be qualified to move up to the next level.

Finally, clients who are capable of more independent work are assigned to service contracts or community job placement programs. These men and women are given more advanced vocational training in custodial, food service, or retail sales and service jobs, earning a paycheck while they learn. They are employed under the auspices of one of Opportunity Village's federal, state or local government contracts, or private industry contracts. You'll read more about these in chapter eight.

It's important to point out that no client is ever forced to move up this ladder to a more advanced level. If a client has progressed to the point where he or she could advance, they are considered for "promotion." However, their personal preferences, the opinion of their chief caregivers, and the advice of staff that work most closely with them are all factors that are also taken into consideration.

Opportunity Village is not just about vocational training for people with disabilities. It is, first and foremost, about improving the lives of its clients. In many cases, this improvement may take the form of achieving a better paying position, at a more functional level, and when that is the case, the client is given every chance to succeed with Opportunity Village's help. But in just as many cases, what the client wants most out of life is simply to retain the comfort level he has achieved working with a group of friends and staffers who love and support him. A better job isn't what will make him happy; the status quo will. And so he is allowed to stay in the same position, and at the same level, for his entire life if that's what makes him happy. Being happy is what it's all about, not earning the biggest possible paycheck.

This philosophy has often put Opportunity Village at odds with the Association of Retarded Citizens (ARC), the national group with which Opportunity Village is affiliated.

ARC's belief is that people with intellectual disabilities are best served by being forced up the ladder of achievement, with the ultimate goal being total inclusion in the community. Opportunity Village is not willing to follow that path if it conflicts with the emotional well being of its clients.

"There seem to be waves that go through this movement," said Ed Guthrie, Opportunity Village's Executive Director. "Everybody has to be in an institution; then everybody has to be in a group home, and nobody can be in an institution. Then everybody has to be fully included in a normal classroom, then everybody should be in a special school."

"I'm a market-based capitalist when it comes to providing services," he said. "You tell me what you want and I'll try to get you the best services I can."

Guthrie said there are well meaning people on both sides of the argument, and that there are no easy answers. However, there is currently no appetite at Opportunity Village to change the "client well being comes first" mentality.

♥ ♥ ♥

Nathaniel Schaus was a normal, fun loving eight year old kid who loved sports and outdoor activities. But in 1988, while on a rock climbing excursion in Red Rock Canyon, he slipped and plunged eighty feet onto the rocks below. He suffered traumatic brain damage. Today, Schaus has no speech, and is confined to a wheelchair. Feeding tubes, a waste sucking machine and a breathing apparatus keep him alive by performing necessary functions for his wasted body. After more than forty operations, Schaus is about as good as he'll ever get, his mother, Loralie Schaus, admits.

Speaking in a halting voice, she said, "Cognitively, he is very high functioning. He's a young man with above average intelligence who is trapped in a useless body."

Nathaniel graduated from Clark High School in 2000, a miracle in itself and testament to how far public education has come in the last fifty years.

"But all of a sudden," his mother said, "there was nothing for him." So he spent the next year at home with his mom, and she admitted, "my son was deteriorating, and so was his mother."

Then she discovered Project PRIDE at Opportunity Village. One of the organization's newest programs, Project PRIDE is a therapeutic day program for young people with profound physical or intellectual disabilities who require round-the-clock care and monitoring. These are the intellectually and physically handicapped, the most fragile members of our society. They require assistance to perform life's most basic functions, like breathing, eating and toileting.

The program's staff to client ratio of two-to-one makes it possible to provide individualized therapy programs for each participant, allowing each one to get the most out of life. Staff is also augmented by volunteers who work with the Project PRIDE clients, and by medical personnel who come in to evaluate the clients on a regular basis, or simply to volunteer their time.

Physical and occupational therapists also come in to instruct staff in different kinds of range of motion exercises, and other therapies that are needed to work with each individual client.

"This is the only place that offers services now that can give Nathaniel's life meaning and balance," Loralie Schaus says flatly. "He wants to have purpose;

Opportunity Village is not just about vocational training . . . first and foremost, about improving the lives of its clients.

Director of client services Maria Rodriguez reads to Project PRIDE clients Naomi Hau and Nathaniel Schaus.

he wants to do something that is of value, and the staff works very hard to find things he can accomplish . . . to help him do the things he *can* do."

"The difference in him now, compared to before he had anyplace to go, is amazing," she said.

Project PRIDE (the PRIDE stands for People's Right to Independence with Dignity and Equality) was started by three parents in 2000 when they couldn't find anyplace for their children who were forced out of the school system at age twenty-two.

They decided to start their own program, but soon discovered that it was a more involved and costly enterprise than they were equipped to undertake. So they asked Opportunity Village if they would take the program on, and see to its funding.

One of those founding parents was Lynda Carson, a single parent with three boys. Her youngest son,

Chris, was born in 1977. At birth, his umbilical cord was wrapped around his neck, cutting off oxygen to his brain, and as a baby he had to undergo two serious operations. Today, Carson admits she is not sure which event led to his profound mental and physical disabilities.

Chris attended the John F. Miller School, the School District's special education school that teaches children with the most profound disabilities. About five years before he was to be phased out at twenty-two, the school advised Mrs. Carson to begin thinking about what she would do when he graduated. There were only two options: she could care for Chris herself at home, a 24/7 job that sucks the very marrow out of a caretaker's bones, or she could have him admitted to a nursing home. Neither option held much promise, so

Carson and a few other parents in the same situation decided to take matters into their own hands.

After visiting with officials at Opportunity Village, they began writing the state legislature asking that additional money be set aside to fund a program for their children. While the politicians were still studying the matter, the Opportunity Village board of directors decided to take the program under their wing. They opened a facility near the airport at Patrick and Eastern, and for the first two years they funded it themselves, out of their regular operating expenses. When the Henderson campus opened in 2001, the program transferred there to an area that had been especially built and equipped.

Chris Carson, the young man who initially spurred the idea for Project PRIDE, passed away in November 2001. "For the past few years, I've been healing," Lynda Carson admitted. "It's so difficult to lose a child." She has been asked to serve on the parents committee for the capital campaign to build the southwest campus, and she has accepted the appointment.

Echoing a popular sentiment, Carson said, "Project PRIDE did save my life, and it gave meaning to Chris's last three years."

Today, Project PRIDE, which was one of the earliest programs of its kind in the United States, operates at both the West Oakey campus and the Walters Family Campus in Henderson. In early 2006, West Oakey had seventeen clients and Henderson ten. Maria Rodriguez, Day Training Manager at West Oakey (since, promoted to Director of Program Services for Opportunity Village) and Amanda Shipp who holds the same position in Henderson, are in charge of the program. They anticipate a growing need in the Southern Nevada community for such services, as the population of profoundly handicapped men and women increases in the nation's fastest growing market.

Alvin and Frances Hao also have a child in Project PRIDE. Their daughter Naomi suffers from Rett Syndrome (RS) a neurological disorder seen almost exclusively in females. Girls with RS usually have an early life period of near normal development, up to around six to eighteen months. Then the child begins to lose communication skills and purposeful use of her hands. Seizures and disorganized breathing patterns also begin to occur; the most serious effect is the brain's inability to program the body to perform motor movements.

Like most other people with profound developmental disorders, those with RS are not emotionally vacant. They experience a full range of emotions, have engaging personalities, and enjoy social, educational and recreational activities.

The Haos moved to Las Vegas from Hawaii in 1994 so Naomi could attend the Variety School for Handicapped Children. When she turned twenty-two, and had to exit school, the Haos found Project PRIDE. Naomi was one of the original four participants. "We found another place in town where they would take her," Frances Hao said. "But there, they just sit around all day long with a blanket on their lap."

Not so at Project PRIDE. When you enter the program's large, equipment-filled room, it's abuzz with activity. A red shirted staff member whispers quietly in the ear of one client, who breaks into a smile. Another is reading from a book to a young woman who sits attentively in her wheelchair; while a third attendant swabs out Nathaniel Schaus's mouth when his saliva glands go into overdrive. A woman reaches out and grabs the hand of Maria Rodriguez as we pass by, and she stops to exchange pleasantries.

"Here, they don't talk about disabilities in terms of being a handicap," Loralie Schaus pointed out. "They focus on what each person *can* do, not what they can't do."

A typical day for a client begins when he arrives at Project PRIDE at 7:00 to 8:00 AM, usually after a bus ride that can be as long as two hours. Vital signs are taken and recorded, and a breakfast snack is prepared and fed to each client. Toileting is a regularly occurring event throughout the day. By this time most clients have been in their wheelchair for hours, so they are taken out and comfortably positioned in another chair, or on one of a number of pieces of equipment designed to provide comfort. Each client must be constantly repositioned a throughout the day, and wasted muscles massaged and gently exercised.

At the heart of the program are the two daily activity sessions where the staff and volunteers work one-on-one with each client helping to improve whatever fragile functions their bodies may be able to perform.

"Activities are designed to provide sensory training: audio stimulation, visual stimulation, tactile stimulation, range of motion exercises for those who have contracted limbs . . . it all depends on the client," Rodriguez explained. "Many are non-ambulatory and non-verbal," she said; "and they also need toilet help, feeding help, and help with medications."

"We also use music therapy, adaptive equipment to make them as independent as possible, and other exercises to enhance the skills they do have," Shipp added. "They digress so easily that it's an ongoing challenge."

Lunch and more toileting occurs, then the second activity session. By this time, the day is drawing toward a close, and each client must be prepared for his or her long ride home. Staff will comb each client's hair, brush their teeth, and get them comfortably back in their wheelchair. By 2:00 or 3:00 PM, each client is back on the bus returning home.

There's always time for fun too. "We take them on community outings, and here in the center we have birthday parties and dances in the gym and other fun activities," Amanda Shipp said.

One of the major successes of Opportunity Village comes from the fact that all its clients are able to earn a paycheck. This not only gives each client a great sense of satisfaction and independence, it also makes them wage earning members of society at large, and their work efforts contribute to the organization's high level of self sufficiency.

Surprising at it may first seem, even the clients in Project PRIDE earn a wage.

"This is a relatively new part of the program," Rodriguez admitted. "Parents or caregivers are responsible for paying for transportation to and from Opportunity Village, and it's a cost that's constantly going up for them. We thought this would help defray that cost." These clients are paid only a stipend, simply for their attendance, but it gives them a feeling of independence.

Parents and caregivers are charged nothing for the program. Whatever government funds they may receive — social security payments, Medicaid reimbursements, etc. — they are free to use for the significant at home care that is required of them.

The vast majority of care provided by Project PRIDE is to advance participants' quality of life. But occasionally, a minor miracle occurs, and a client is able to advance to the next stage of rehabilitation. In that rare event, Rodriguez and Shipp admit, it makes all their efforts worthwhile.

"If I hadn't found Project PRIDE," Nathaniel's mother Loralie Schaus said, "I'm not sure that Nathaniel or I — either one of us — would still be alive today."

It's difficult to imagine any higher praise for the program.

♥ ♥ ♥

On that rare occasion when a Project PRIDE client does show enough improvement to advance, they become a member of Project ENABLE, the next rung up the ladder. The stated goal of this program is "to provide the services, support and supervision necessary for people with intellectual disabilities to become active, productive members of our community."

While Project PRIDE serves clients with profound disabilities, Project ENABLE serves people with very severe intellectual disabilities and related behavioral issues.

As you walk from Project PRIDE to Project ENABLE, you're immediately aware of the change.

In the former, there is very little noise. Most of the clients are not vocal, and the loudest sounds you hear are the comforting and soothing words uttered by the staff as they tend to these most fragile clients.

In the latter, on the other hand, your first impression is of noise. At first blush, it appears that chaos reigns, but you'll soon discover that, despite the noise, there is orderliness to what is occurring. Clients mumble and chatter, perhaps even scream out, but this doesn't detract from the training they are undergoing. Here, clients learn through experience, through repetitive motion, rather than through more conventional teaching methods. For the least able of

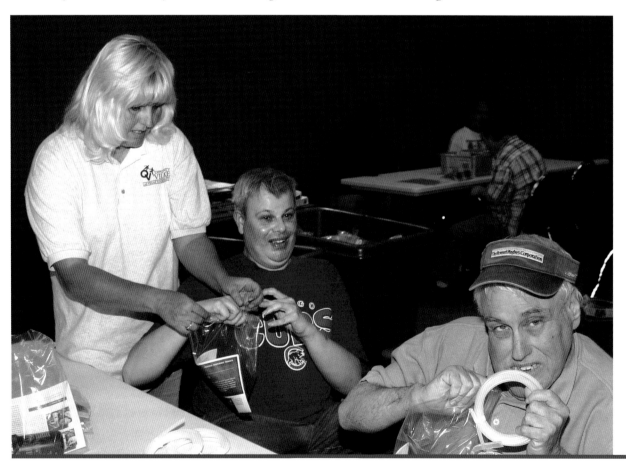

Dixie Fouch helps David Fernandez learn a new skill with a hand-over-hand teaching technique in Project ENABLE, while Vendon Pulsipher waits his turn.

these clients, a process called hand-over-hand training is employed. A staff member physically moves the client's hand through a desired movement hundreds — perhaps even thousands — of times until the client learns the movement.

Project ENABLE clients are taught skills in socialization, communication, self-advocacy, and behavior self-management that are a necessary prerequisite for any future, more advanced vocational training.

For a client to advance to this level, or to be initially placed in the program, they must meet certain criteria. They must be able to handle their basic eating and toileting needs, even if assistance is required, and they must be able to work cooperatively as part of a group. Despite having these basic attributes, they still require direct supervision, which they often rebel against, and they are often unable to communicate their basic needs. They have a long learning curve, and have a great deal of difficulty adjusting to any change. Staffing level in the program varies, from one staff person for every five clients to one staff person for every two clients, depending upon the activity.

One thing that makes these clients the most difficult group to work with is their inability to control behaviors. They may lash out, and they often emit high pitched squeals, grunts, groans and humming sounds. They are the most difficult group to teach and train.

Despite that, they work. The assembly contracts they take on are of the most basic type: one items is stuffed into one bag or envelope. They are also taken out into the community — the job they love best — to distribute flyers door to door. No profit will be realized from these contracts as the required transportation and staffing level is so high. Still, it's a job, and the pride the clients feel receiving a regular paycheck makes it all worthwhile.

♥ ♥ ♥

The next rung up the ladder are the employment training centers, often referred to as sheltered workshops. At Opportunity Village, these come in many forms: assembly and packaging centers, collating and mailing center, the thrift store, the document shredding department and the button shop. Also considered a part of the campus is Opportunity Village's food service training center, in the organization's new, gleaming state of the art kitchen.

Amy Yang is a small, intent woman, with thick glasses perched on the end of her nose; her pretty face is highlighted by the distinctive oval eyes that suggest she is one of the many Down syndrome clients at Opportunity Village. When I first saw her, she was hard at work in the kitchen, one of the five training modules that are part of the Job Discovery Program.

Wielding a small, knife with as much care and delicacy as a brain surgeon, Amy carefully cut onion pieces into small dice. Strangely, I thought, the task didn't seem to be making her tear. Her method was quite unique; I've always made lengthwise cuts through an onion half, then turned it and cut the onion crosswise, watching the small diced pieces fall onto my cutting board. But I soon learned watching Amy that I held no patent on the "correct" way to dice an onion.

Amy had sectioned her onion into a number of unequal chunks before I arrived. Now she carefully pulled each chunk apart, one layer at a time, and began meticulously dicing each single layer with great care. It was obvious that Amy's complete concentration was focused on the job at hand, and she never glanced up as I watched her perform the delicate operation. Done my way, the chore would have taken about thirty seconds, while it took Amy about fifteen minutes, but I had to remind myself that my analytical thinking missed the point completely.

When Amy finished, the kitchen supervisor, Mr. Jose, walked over and admired the small pile of diced onion, and whispered a genuine compliment for a job well done. Amy's smile beamed so brightly that I swear it reflected light off the stainless steel equipment that surrounded her in the kitchen. The warmth and pride she exuded for a job well done was as sincere and as well earned as Wolfgang Puck may have felt as he pulled a perfectly risen Belgian chocolate soufflé from the oven.

Quite frankly, I was overwhelmed with pride for her, and quickly wiped a tear from my own eye.

The Job Discovery Program is a unique partnership between the organization and the Clark County School District. It was developed to give eleventh and twelfth grade students with disabilities the chance to learn various job skills, and experience the workplace before they come out of high school.

"Most kids hold a number of jobs while they're in school, or during the summer," said chief development officer Linda Smith. "But our population . . . they can seldom be paper boys, or work at McDonalds. So we wanted to give them that exposure to work while they were still in school, so when they graduate the transition to the workplace is smoother for them."

Job Discovery has six different training modules, including the food service training in the kitchen. Within Opportunity Village's facilities, there is also training in the employment training centers: packaging and assembly, collating and mailing, and custodial; and there is retail training at the Thrift Store. Outside the organization's facilities, there is animal

Left: *Tylan Lucero received his training as part of the Job Discovery program.*
Right: *Jose Zaragosa (left) and Amy Yang were two successful members of the Job Discovery program.*

care training at the Lied Animal Shelter, working with senior citizens at the Henderson Senior Center, and childcare training at the Variety Day Home.

A student — one enrolled in special education — must be between the ages seventeen and twenty-one in order to participate in the program. This training replaces the student's normal school work, but each participant has already received their diploma, although they have remained in school as allowed by the federal Individuals with Disabilities Education Act.

Each student who is enrolled will spend forty-five days training in each of the six work disciplines, for a total commitment of about eight months. Executive Director Ed Guthrie calls the Job Discovery program a training and assessment program. "The whole time the training is going on," he said, "the student is assessing us, and we're assessing him."

In the past the program was able to accommodate thirty-four to thirty-eight students at a time, but currently Clark County School District has agreed to expand the program to sixty participants.

At the end of the training program, it is intended that the student will have selected an area of vocational inter-est. Following graduation from high school, he or she can apply to join one of Opportunity Village's work programs, or seek employment in his selected field in the community. Opportunity Village assists in job placement and provides follow-along services to help with the transition and protect the student's safety and well-being.

♥ ♥ ♥

One of Opportunity Village's oldest business ventures is the button shop at the West Oakey campus. Here, lapel buttons and badges have been manufactured since 1975.

Mac Sebald, the Director of Employment Training Center Operations, oversees the button shop, as well as the document shredding business and both employment training centers for Opportunity Village.

Mac Seabald, director of employment training center operations, and new ventures manager Laura D'Amore, watch Ray Dortiak as he works an assembly contract.

A relative newcomer to the organization, Seabald, an industrial engineer, brings a wealth of private industry manufacturing experience to his job.

"We have two kinds of customers. One gives us an ongoing contract, like Harrahs Entertainment or The Bellagio, and another customer gives us one shot deals, maybe a couple thousand pieces," Sebald explained. These jobs, he said, could be stuffing envelopes, assembling items like a resilient sound isolation clip, or any number of other diverse jobs.

How is this different, Sebald is asked, from managing a manufacturing plant in private industry? "It's no different," he said. "You're going to make things at a certain pace, and that's what you plan for. The fact that your individuals are disabled just makes it better," he smiled. "It's really cool working with these individuals."

Sebald sees opportunity in the button shop. Currently, the shop only has equipment for making two different sizes of buttons, but he has recently ordered new equipment that will manufacture three other sizes and shapes. "We're going to get an ad on the internet, and send out mailers, and see if we can grow that business," he said.

Opportunity Village's button shop had its fifteen minutes of fame when it twice received contracts to produce political buttons for presidential campaigns. The first order came in 1984 and called for the manufacture of a quarter of a million buttons for the Ronald Reagan – George Bush re-election campaign. Reagan and Bush won that election, and soon after, Opportunity Village received a letter from the White House:

> With heartfelt thanks, I congratulate you, the staff, and the members of Opportunity Village Association for Retarded Citizens for your hard work and dedication in producing our 1984 Presidential Re-Election Campaign Buttons, especially on such short notice.
>
> I truly and personally appreciate your help.
>
> You have become a role model for the handicapped across our great nation, showing our citizens that having a disability does not prevent an individual from doing quality work.
>
> — God Bless you all.
>
> Ronald W. Reagan
> President
> Unites States of America

1984 newspaper ad for Opportunity Village's button shop.

Eight years later, on February 6, 1992, President George Bush, announced that he was making a stop in Las Vegas as part of a cross country trip to promote his health care proposals. To the chagrin of the State Republican party, President Bush eschewed their invitation to speak at a Republican fundraising rally, and announced instead that he would make only two stops in Las Vegas. His second stop, he said, would be to the University Medical Center to discuss his health care initiatives with the medical personnel, and his first stop? He announced he would visit Opportunity Village on West Oakey Boulevard.

Amidst tight security, President Bush and his entourage arrived at the Emplyment Training Center and were greeted by hundreds of clients and staff members wearing "Welcome President Bush" lapel buttons. The clients were beside themselves with excitement. The President shook hands, signed autographs, exchanged pleasantries and passed out keepsakes to everyone. The next day, the *Las Vegas Review-Journal* captured a few of the comments: "He dresses nice;" "He's doing a good job;" and, "I bet he has a headache every night."

So impressed with what he saw was President Bush that a month later his office placed an order for 100,000 buttons for the 1992 Bush – Quayle re-election campaign. Perhaps they should have ordered more buttons; the Bush – Quayle ticket lost in the November election.

Whether or not the Opportunity Village button shop can recapture its illustrious past is yet to be seen, but don't count it out, according to Mac Sebald. The button shop has never provided training for too many people, and in recent years the emphasis has been placed on those areas that serve the most clients. But Seabald sees dollar signs in the button shop, money that could be put to good use in other areas. So with the flexibility possible with the new equipment, his

President George Bush visits Opportunity Village.

own sales force, and his expanded marketing plans, Seabald is confident the button shop will again shine.

♥ ♥ ♥

In the far southeastern corner of Clark County lies the city of Henderson. Once a sleepy little town made up of remnants of the World War II era Basic Magnesium, Inc. plant, today the city is the second largest in the state of Nevada, trailing only Las Vegas in population. For the past few years, the city's growth has surpassed even that of its more famous neighbor. Today, 250,000 people call Henderson home.

With that growth has come the same problems associated with any growing city. Among them has been the growth of the city's population of people with intellectual disabilities. Twenty years ago, a resident living in Henderson could take a thirty minute bus ride and arrive at Opportunity Village's West Oakey campus. Today, that same bus trip takes up to ninety minutes, thanks to the area's clogged streets and freeways.

Opportunity Village executives saw this problem coming on years ago, and began planning how to combat it. Selma Bartlett, a longtime Henderson community advocate, saw the problem coming too, and jumped into the fray. Working with Basic Management, Inc. (BMI) a large Henderson based land management company, Bartlett began advocating for a land donation. BMI officials eventually donated a 2.16 acre parcel of land to Opportunity Village for a Henderson area facility.

In 2000, the Walters Family Campus opened on East Lake Mead Parkway in Henderson. An attractive facility fronted by gently curving desert red sandstone blocks, the 22,500 square foot facility today serves 120 clients every day who live in the valley's southeastern quadrant. The building contains a huge employment training center, the organization's document destruction business, Project PRIDE and Project ENABLE facilities, and offices.

The center in Henderson is very similar to the one at the West Oakey campus. It's a very large, industrial looking room, with supporting girders, air conditioning ducts and other construction elements visible high overhead. Hanging from the ceiling at regular intervals are long, heavy duty yellow electrical cords, just out of reach but ready to be lowered when power is needed at any specific workstation. The room is lined with long rows of twelve foot worktables, with comfortable chairs on each side. Here, dozens of clients sit busily involved at their tasks.

One of the contracts being filled during our visit was for Harrahs Entertainment. Small packages containing sugar, artificial sweetener, creamer and a stirring stick were being assembled and stuffed into small plastic bags. At the end of each row of tables one of the bright yellow electrical cords provided power to a sealing machine that put the finishing touch on each small coffee condiment package.

Some clients assembled their packages quickly with long practiced movements; others have a cardboard schematic in front of them with a boxed drawing of each element that goes into the package. Slowly,

Rodney Newton works in Henderson's Walters Family Campus Employment Training Center.

methodically, these clients examined each individual piece very carefully, turning it over in their hand and studying it intently against the schematic, before carefully inserting it into the plastic bag. These clients receive less pay for their efforts than their other workmates, but for each client, regardless of his pace, there will be a paycheck come payday.

The Harrahs coffee condiment packages that are assembled here in Henderson, Nevada, will go into every room of every Harrahs resort throughout the entire country. It is a very substantial contract, one of the best Opportunity Village has.

Another group was assembling eating utensil packages for a cutlery contract with Host International. A plastic knife and fork were carefully wrapped up in a paper napkin, and a green self-sticking paper band held the package together. As I watched, a young woman approached me. Her badge told me her name was Cecilia. She is perhaps five feet tall, with her right leg heavily encased in a rigid iron brace. Dark brown hair cut in a fashionable bob encircled a happy, smiling face. At first I had to strain to understand Cecelia, but then I understood.

"Come with me. I show you."

At her workstation, Cecilia slowly assembled a package for my benefit, watching me intently to make sure I understood. "You do it now," she told me; so I began. Unfortunately, I did not position the two utensils at the proper angle across the napkin, and my package looked awkward and bulky. "No! No! No!" she scolded me. "Again." On the second try, I got it right, and Cecelia clapped happily. I thanked her for the lesson, and she beamed at me.

Because both the Harrahs and Host International contracts are ongoing agreements, these are the main contracts that are necessary to keep the eighty Henderson Employment Training Center clients busy. At the West Oakey campus, on the other hand, where around 180 clients are in the employment training center, it isn't unusual to have a dozen different contracts going on at any given time.

During a recent visit, the West Oakey clients were busily assembling a resilient sound isolation clip, a strange looking metal and plastic contraption that eliminates the need for soundproofing walls and ceilings in rooms that generate a lot of noise, like practice rooms for a rock band. The devices instead are fastened on the wall's studs before regular wallboard is installed. The manufacturer of the product, an Oregon based company, says in their slogan, "We don't build buildings, we just make them quiet!" It must work well, as Opportunity Village enjoys a large contract assembling the devices.

Over the years, the Employemt Training Centers have fulfilled some very unusual contracts. They've pasted the center sticker on thousands of casino gaming chips, and they've put labels on bags of toffee. They've assembled holiday gift baskets, and boiled and decorated thousands of Easter eggs. But perhaps the most unusual job they've ever performed — and one that brought them notoriety for more than a quarter-century — was the production of the Elvis scarves.

By the late 1960s, Elvis was performing most of his concerts in his custom made sequined jumpsuits. The costume had become quite elaborate, and it included a silk scarf The King wore around his neck. In 1969, while he was performing at the Las Vegas Hilton, a new tradition was born when Elvis tore the scarf from around his neck, wiped the sweat from his brow, and threw the scarf into the audience where hundreds of wildly screaming fans fought for the prize. Never one to miss an opportunity, Elvis's scarf routine became a staple at every concert — not just one scarf, mind you, but several dozen sweat soaked scarves would be flung into the audience.

Elvis's manager, Colonel Tom Parker, was familiar with Opportunity Village, and he came to the organization and asked if they could provide the scarves. And so a legend was born.

Shiela Siegel has been a client with Opportunity Village for more than thirty years. It was Siegel's job to sew the scarves. Some of them Elvis used during his concerts, others were shipped to gift shops around the world for sale to crazed fans. Clients also put ribbons on Elvis's signature stuffed hound dogs, and the button shop made "Elvis Live at the Hilton" buttons.

Siegel still fondly remembers her brush with fame. It is memorialized by a framed Elvis photo with one of his scarves in the lobby at West Oakey, and even after all these years Siegel still enjoys her job. "This place is nice," she beams. "I have a good job and good pay."

In a large room, adjoining the center in Henderson, one of Opportunity Village's most promising business ventures hums along. Admittance to the room is through a coded entry door. Inside, staff supervisors and busy clients hustled from place to place, pushing large blue trash bins, each filled with detritus of modern corporate America. This is the document destruction business, the second largest such enterprise in Southern Nevada, where four staffers and thirteen clients are employed.

The focal point in the room is a long, conveyor fed machine that does the heavy work in the operation. The trash filled bins are first dumped onto the sorting table where clients separate the paper from other, non-shredable items like plastic and cardboard. These bins are from a number of hotel/casino clients, and from Wells Fargo Bank, that use Opportunity Village's document destruction services exclusively. One of the biggest reasons is honesty.

One casino told a company manager that before hiring Opportunity Village, they had never had any money returned that may have found its way accidentally into the trash. Opportunity Village returns about $30,000 of errant cash a year to its customers. For the clients, it's a big game. Whenever cash is found — occasionally a full green canvas cash bag has ended up on the conveyor — the client excitedly waves it in the air and shouts, "Pizza! Pizza!" Everyone joins in, "Pizza!" A supervisor claims the cash, and the whole crew gets pizza for lunch the following day. Small denomination coins are put into a large jar at the end of the conveyor, and that money is used to buy soft drinks for the crew.

From the sorting table the paper refuse goes to the next station. Here, books and notebooks must be torn apart by hand, heavy metal clips removed, and everything fed into the giant shredding machine. At the far end of the room, the material comes out as a huge brick of tightly compacted shredded paper, which is automatically tied and moved by forklift onto waiting trucks. Opportunity Village sells the waste paper to a recycler; they also sell the cardboard and the plastic, and even bag and sell the metal clips. Nothing with value is wasted. The business shreds an average of eight tons of paper documents daily.

Every day, Opportunity Village trucks pick up and deliver the trash bins to customers throughout Clark County. Leading banks, gaming properties, federal, state and local government entities, medi-

> *Opportunity Village returns about $30,000 of errant cash a year to its customers.*

Beth Cook shows famed NASCAR driver Kyle Petty how its done when he visited the West Oakey Employment Training Center.

Shiela Siegel (left) a veteran client of Opportunity Village's employment training center, admires a framed plaque honoring her work in making the famed Elvis Presley scarves in the late 1970s.

cal, dental, insurance and legal businesses all have contracts with the document destruction department. Opportunity Village is AAA certified under the National Association for Information Destruction, the trade group representing the industry.

Not too many years ago, Opportunity Village waited for employment training center contracts to come to them. As related in chapter six, that worked well for years. "Hire the Handicapped" was a great slogan, and it resonated in the community. No longer. Now it's up to the organization to go out and find profitable contracts to keep the employment training centers busy.

Laura D'Amore was the general manager of the employment training centers for four years, so when top management wanted to find someone who understood the operation, and had the personality for sales, they tapped her as the sales manager. "I prefer sales and marketing manager," D'Amore said. "It better reflects what we do." She has one other salesperson in the department, and it's their job to see that the many and varied employment training center operations have a constant supply of contracts with outside firms to keep them busy.

This new emphasis on sales has paid off. "We used to take whatever came in," D'Amore said, "but now we have regular meetings to decide which contracts

James Ruggles boxes brand new pails in the West Oakey employment training center for one of the group's many contracts.

to accept and which ones to pass on." The success has come through hard work, competitive pricing, and a great product. The Opportunity Village clients who actually fulfill the contracts are diligent workers with excellent attendance records, and they really enjoy the repetitive, routine work that is required on almost every job.

"We can go to a small manufacturer who has hand work done on an assembly line," D'Amore pointed out; "and we can tell him we'll replace his $14 an hour labor at a substantial savings."

By growing the business, Opportunity Village has also improved the lives of the clients who train or work in the employment training center operations. D'Amore pointed out that just a few years ago, these clients were earning only a stipend — $20 to $30 a week — because there were so few contracts. Today, the some clients earn $200 to $300 a week, while the average is about $150 a week.

♥ ♥ ♥

The 900 block of South Main Street, only about a half mile south of downtown's Glitter Gulch, would never be confused with Rodeo Drive in Beverly Hills. Auto repair shops, used furniture stores, and bail bondsmen share the neighborhood with adult book stores, secondhand mattress shops and a palm and tarot card reading studio. If you allow your eyes to stray over the top of the gaudily painted one and two story buildings that line the street, however, you will see on the horizon brand new multi-storied office buildings and urban residential/retail complexes that are ever so slowly encroaching on the rundown commercial neighborhood that is South Main Street.

Spreading along almost an entire block of the street is the one story Opportunity Village Thrift Store. At one time this was the vocational training center and administrative offices for the entire organization. It began with one small building purchased in the late 1960s. Then the small store next door was added, then the one next to that, where a small thrift store was opened. Today, the entire structure occupies the space that once housed about a half-dozen different small businesses, and it's now all one big thrift store. The façade of the building, painted a bright blue to blend in with the rest of the neighborhood, ties it all together.

With the encroachment of urban development, the site is becoming more valuable every day. Opportunity Village has already turned down a $5,000,000 offer for the property.

Inside, the store is a happy beehive of activity. A flyer at the front door announces the month's sales events: "Two for Tuesday," a two-for-one day for sweaters; "St. Paddy's Weekend Sale," where all green-tagged items will be fifty-percent off; and "Sofa Day," when every sofa in the store is half off. The interior walls of all the original stores have never been removed, so the store is a maze of separate rooms joined by open archways. There's a men's department, a ladies department, and an electronics department; a book room, a housewares room, a room of toys and a huge furniture room. There are also two large processing rooms, where donations are received, separated, and prepared for sale.

Between some of the rooms, there are still remnants of an earlier era: a wide alley, and a large area simply called the yard, open air areas where donated goods that are not up to snuff are stacked sky high awaiting either a special sale or a trip to the public dump.

The *Clark County Yellow Pages* lists dozens of thrift shops — many are along the same South Main Street corridor — and most have the names of local charities appended to them. Donations of used clothing and merchandise are constantly being solicited of the community, and many of the organizations have drop-off points around the area. But the fact is Opportunity Village is one of very few not-for-profits that actually operates its own thrift store. Most of the others are run by private enterprise, under the name of the charity, and the charity only receives about eight to ten percent of the profits. At the Opportunity Village Thrift Store, which grosses about a $1 million a year, all the profits go back into supporting the group's programs.

Two of Opportunity Village's most senior staffers, in terms of employment time, work at the Thrift Store. Yvonne Givens, started with the organization in 1978, while Sandra Brown started in 1979.

Givens began as a cashier, but also did window displays, stocking, assisting customers, and any other duty asked of her. Brown began in the processing center, where donated merchandise first arrives at the store and is readied for sale. Givens is quick to admit that as time passed they began to think of the store as home. It was their challenge to make it successful, and the clients who work and train there became their friends. She shared a story that exemplified their pride in making the store the very best they could.

"In the 1980s, Levis were hot," Givens recalled. "A few Levis had red threading running through them, while most others had green threading. We discov-

Sandra Brown (from left) Ann Clemons and Yvonne Givens have all worked at the Main Street Thrift Store for more than a quarter-century.

ered that the ones with the red threading were worth more money for some reason, so we'd spend days searching for the ones with red."

The ladies soon discovered that the green-threaded Levis could be sold for $10 a pair, but the red-threaded one would bring $20.

"It was a fun thing to do," Givens smiled, "but we made hundreds of dollars more by pricing the Levis correctly."

In the early days, the thrift store was run differently. The store was broken down into a number of small boutique shops: antiques and collectibles, upscale women's wear, furniture, toys and games, and so on. This was before interior doors were cut between the individual stores, so each boutique had its own entrance right off the street, its own sales people and its own cashier. Eventually, the boutiques had to give way to reduce redundant expenses, but Givens recalled those early days fondly, especially the secondhand clothing fashion shows staged by the Vanguard Club that will be discussed in chapter ten.

Yard sales were another popular event. Items that hadn't sold in a reasonable time were moved out into the open air yard, and every Tuesday a giant yard sale auction was held. "People began lining up at 7:30 in the morning," Givens said, "and there would be a line of cars blocks long waiting to get in. People loved it!"

Today, Givens says about eight out of every ten customers are repeat customers. Included in that group are a number of swap meet dealers who come in every day for hours, scouring the merchandise for anything new that may have come in. About thirty percent of all business comes from them, she said.

As for staff, there are fifteen Opportunity Village employees at the thrift store, and about two dozen clients. Many of the clients have been at the store for a long time, two for more than thirty-five years, and these men and women love "their" store. Given a chance to move up to a work contract with better pay and employee benefits, most refuse to budge.

Yvonne Givens and Sandra Brown are very proud of those clients who have taken the risk however. Some have gone on to good jobs in retailing in the community, due to their training at the thrift store.

"We have people at Target, and at Wal-Mart," Givens said. "The majority of our folks who have left did not come back; they're still out in the workforce," she said proudly.

Clients working at the thrift store still socialize at the West Oakey campus with the other clients. "They're not missing the dances," Givens said. But there are also birthday parties, incentive award parties, productivity and attendance presentations right at the thrift store, and the clients love the festivities.

All in all, the Opportunity Village Thrift Store on West Main Street may not be as posh as Rodeo Drive, but for its staff, its clients and its customers, with an apology to Disneyland, it's still the happiest place on earth.

With their new emphasis on competing more aggressively in the for-profit marketplace, Opportunity Village is making a name for itself in the Southern Nevada business community.

An early Thrift Store ad for "Oh! Vees," Opportunity Village's own collection of "recycled" designer jeans.

The early thrift shop was divided into a number of specialty boutiques, like this toy store.

*Dottie Kish enjoys her job as
a certified kitchen helper.*

CHAPTER EIGHT

Employment:
It's Cool to Have a Job!

It's very easy to confuse the training programs with the employment programs within Opportunity Village. Some of the differences were discussed in chapter six. The Employment Training Centers at the West Oakey and Henderson campuses, the thrift store, the button shop, the document destruction business, and the food service training in the kitchen are all part of the vocational training programs, or sheltered workshops. Although this is considered vocational training, clients earn a piece-rate wage while involved in these activities.

Those clients who have both the ability and the desire to earn a higher wage and gain more independence move to the work service contract program. This program includes all the government and private industry contracts Opportunity Village operates in the community. Most of these jobs are custodial and food service, although the organization has recently added a small grounds keeping division that they expect to grow.

Opportunity Village's Chief Operating Officer, and the man responsible for all the group's service contract work, as well as the thrift store, is Kurt Weinrich.

Weinrich moved to Las Vegas from San Diego as a teenager in the early 1980s to enter the veterinary profession. However, he soon found a flaw in his plan: "I discovered the blood and guts of being a veterinarian were not going to be for me," he smiled. Instead, he joined the newly opened Sam's Town Hotel & Casino, and spent the next twenty years moving up the ladder in the food and beverage industry with the Boyd Group.

The Las Vegas hotel food and beverage directors' organization has been one of Opportunity Village's most stalwart supporters for more than fifty years. It was only natural therefore that they would come on board early when the Magical Forest, the group's Christmas holiday extravaganza, was born. As a board member of the food and beverage group, Weinrich found himself volunteering to head up their Magical Forest participation. Over the next four years, he became steadily more involved, and when Opportunity Village began pitching for a huge food service contract at Nellis Air Force Base, Weinrich became a key player as a volunteer in obtaining the contract.

Kurt Weinrich was also at a career crossroads. So when he was offered the chance to join Opportunity Village as Chief Operating Officer, he jumped at it. That was in September 2001, and he admits he has never regretted the move.

"I've always felt the Opportunity Village mission is very compelling," Weinrich said, "but the challenge of my position has been to bring some corporate structure to the business side of the organization."

The Nellis contract was a $3.5 million contract, and it helped launched the service contract business in a big way. Now, Weinrich said, his big challenge is in new business development.

However, that challenge is a two-edged sword. New business means more job openings, a good thing, but it is becoming more difficult to recruit people to fill the jobs, a bad thing. Weinrich pointed out that only the highest functioning clients can be employed on the service contracts, and that's where the shortage occurs. It's a competitive thing too, he admits. As recently as five years ago, clients with only forty to fifty percent functionality were being employed on service contracts, but in order to compete in today's business environment, that's no longer good enough.

This new climate is a result of Opportunity Village's ascension into the business world. In the old days, the group was often granted small contracts by companies simply trying to be good citizens by hiring people with disabilities. Now, however, with all the large contracts they administer, Opportunity Village is expected to provide service on a par with private industry.

So far, that's worked in the group's favor, because the service provided by its clients is actually better and more reliable than that of most of its competitors. A custodial worker earning, say, nine dollars an hour, is often not a fulfilled, contented employee. But his disabled coworker is a happy, satisfied individual who considers himself very fortunate to have such a fine job that pays such an extravagant wage. So the problem is to find enough workers with disabilities to fill all the available slots.

All of Opportunity Village's federal work service contracts come about as a result of a government-sponsored program called JWOD. In 1938, under President Franklin Roosevelt, Congress passed the Wagner-O'Day Act, designed to provide employment for the blind by allowing them to manufacture mops and brooms to sell to the Federal Government. In 1971, under the leadership of Senator Jacob Javits, Congress amended the act to allow all people with severe disabilities to provide products and services to the Federal Government. The new law became known as JWOD, after the three sponsors.

Today, JWOD works through a central nonprofit agency called the National Institute to Serve the Handicapped, or NISH, which in turn works with local not for profits like Opportunity Village, to place Federal contracts that have been earmarked for workers with disabilities (called Federal contract set asides.) This program has often been referred to as an example of government at its very best.

Early in 2006, Opportunity Village had an enviable list of contracts they service. One JWOD contract alone, the Nellis Air Force Base contract, which is the only food service contract at the time, requires between fifty-five and ninety clients, depending upon the functional level of the staff at any given time. This number is augmented by approximately twenty non-disabled back-fill employees and supervisory staff. The contract involves feeding all of Nellis's military and civilian staff, which came to a whopping total of over 400,000 meals in 2005 alone. Opportunity Village's clients duties include set ups, serving, bussing, and cleanup for all meals. Cooks employed by Opportunity Village, do the food preparation.

Clients who work on the Nellis contract have undergone their training while working side by side with the high school students in the Job Discovery program, in Opportunity Village's state of the art kitchen on West Oakey.

On January 25, 1941, Las Vegas Mayor John Russell signed the paper that deeded to the U.S. Army Quartermaster Corps a large chunk of arid desert land eight miles north of the city. War was on the horizon, and the Army wanted to build and operate a gunnery school on the desolate stretch of desert to train aerial gunners for combat. The only thing on the property, besides rattlesnakes and cactus, was a dirt runway used by Western Air Express, a water well, and a small operations shack.

The Nellis contract was a $3.5 million contract, and it helped launched the service contract business in a big way.

Today, that gunnery school has become Nellis Air Force Base. It is part of the U.S. Air Force's Air Combat Command, known in military circles as the "Home of the Fighter Pilot." Nearly 10,000 military and civilian personnel comprise the Nellis' workforce, making it one of the largest employers in Southern Nevada.

Opportunity Village feeds them all. The Nellis work service contract began in 2001.

Opportunity Village personnel service four dining rooms. These are not the mess halls of the old days that many remember; instead, today they are attractive restaurants. The Mountain View Inn and the Red Horse Inn serve meals twenty-four hours a day, while the Crosswinds and the Flight Kitchen operate on more limited hours.

Opportunity Village operates three shifts daily at Nellis: a nine AM to four PM shift, a four PM to one AM shift, and a four AM to eleven AM shift. There is an on site service coordinator who is responsible for advocating for the handicapped clients on all three shifts.

One of the clients who has worked on the Nellis food service contract since it began in 2001 is Jamie Harvey. A tall, trim, thirty-five-year old man with thinning black hair, Harvey moved to Las Vegas with his mother from New York City in 1995. Before finding Opportunity Village a couple of years later, Harvey says, "I was pushing carts inside a grocery store, but I didn't like it."

Harvey began his Opportunity Village career in one of the employment training centers where he assembled buckets at a wage of $5 an hour. When asked how he liked the job, he simply rolled his eyes and said, "It was OK, I guess." But Harvey wanted to earn more money, and he wasn't afraid of tackling new challenges. He progressed to a janitorial crew at the employment training center where he received custodial training, then joined a crew working under a private service contract at the American Nevada Corporation. "I cleaned parking lots," Harvey proudly stated, "and I got a good raise in pay."

When the Nellis contract was obtained — as a JWOD contract, it mandates hourly wages that are normally higher that those paid for private industry contracts — Harvey again requested a transfer. His service coordinator and his supervisors were quick to recommend him, and today, Harvey earns $8.62 an hour working in the Crosswinds dining room. On this day he was washing pots and pans, but he says proudly that he can handle any of the jobs: bussing tables, washing dishes, cleaning bathrooms, or anything else asked of him.

"I like working," Harvey said. "I work hard, but I like it." He also likes his crew members, and the Air Force men and women who he calls friends.

Harvey and his mother live close by, but he is hopeful of getting his own apartment someday if he can afford it. But he feels a very strong responsibility for helping out his mother financially. "I make more than my mom," he said, "and I have to help her with her payments."

Harvey also had a girlfriend. He looks down sheepishly when he says it, but with a warm smile on his face. "Her name is Dorothy," he tells me. Dorothy lives close to Harvey, and works at the Opportunity Village Thrift Store downtown. Together, they attend the Opportunity Village dances, go to movies and watch TV. He also likes to bowl, and play basketball and baseball.

Life is good for Jamie Harvey. He doesn't take it for granted though. He's obviously a man who wants to make as much of himself as possible, and he doesn't mind working hard for it. He's the kind of fellow you'd like to have for a friend, or as a next door neighbor.

❤ ❤ ❤

The budding grounds keeping business includes servicing contracts at the Federal Foley Building in downtown Las Vegas, and at the visitor's center at Red Rock Canyon National Conservation Area outside of the city. Both of these grounds keeping contracts are adjuncts to custodial contracts at the same facilities, but Kurt Weinrich believes eventually the organization will begin securing standalone grounds keeping contracts.

> *"I like working,"
> Harvey said. "I work
> hard, but I like it."*

It is in the custodial area, however, where Opportunity Village really shines. *The Workplace*, NISH's monthly magazine, praised the organization, writing, "Opportunity Village is in a league of its own when it comes to promoting its abilities, accomplishment and the Javits-Wagner-O'Day Act . . ."

JWOD custodial contracts include the Foley Federal Building, twelve Veterans Administration clinics in Southern Nevada, the Bureau of Reclamation's office building, and the Department of Energy office building.

Local government and private industry custodial contracts include the organization's largest custodial customer, over 700,000 square feet of office space at the multi-building Clark County Government Center. There are also contracts with the ten story Clark Building, the Boulder City government municipal offices and a handful of other office and professional buildings.

One of the group's newest and most promising custodial contracts is with McCarran International Airport. Opportunity Village recently received a small contract to service the restrooms in Concourse C for Southwest Airlines, a small beginning for what could eventually become a significant piece of business.

Elio Ramirez is Kurt Weinrich's Director of Service Contracts, and the man most often on the front line between clients and customers. He has worked his way up through the ranks from direct service staff to his present position.

"We've had a three or four year relationship with Clark County," Ramirez said, "and they recommended us to the airport. They told us, 'here's a small piece of business; show us what you can do.'"

♥ ♥ ♥

The JWOD custodial contract for cleaning twelve Veterans Administration clinics in Southern Nevada is overseen by Gwendolyn Briggs. She joined Opportunity Village four years ago as a housekeeper, or custodial worker, as a back fill employee. "It was a second job," she said. "I was a single parent and I needed the money." Briggs moved up the ladder quickly, from housekeeper to lead housekeeper, then to supervisor, and finally to Director of Environmental Services for VA of Southern Nevada, where she oversees the entire VA contract.

One of Briggs' own lead workers is Nehemiah Gipson, twenty-one, from Pine Bluff, Arkansas. Gipson and his mom moved to Las Vegas in 1996, and he entered Opportunity Village as a client three years ago in the custodial training program. But Nehemiah wanted more for himself. "I had a baby coming, and I really needed a good job," he said. Through hard work and persistence, he got promoted to a work service contract, then to lead person on his crew. Today, Gipson is lead worker on the floor crew, and he has two other older, more experienced men under his supervision.

"I work as hard as everybody else on the crew, because the floors are my responsibility," Gipson boasted. "I have to make sure the floors get done well." And he does, according to his boss, Gwen Briggs. I witnessed that myself.

Gipson led me to one of the VA clinics where he and his crew were working. As we entered, he met one of his crew who was on a break. The man had a very worried look on his face, and he pointed to a large gray spot on the linoleum floor, just inside the door. Almost as if the spot was mocking them, the two men got down on their knees and began rubbing at it to see if it would go away. When it did, they both smiled and rose. Even though the spot had obviously been made after that section of floor had been cleaned, Gipson and his team members were not going to let it go uncorrected. Such is the concern these men have for their job.

"I'm very proud of Nehemiah," Briggs said.

Gwen Briggs and Nehemiah Gipson have at least two things in common. First, they both love their work. "I love my job," Nehemiah said. "Opportunity Village has been very good to me." Gwen echoed that sentiment: "I love working for Opportunity Village. It's a great company."

The second thing they have in common is the example both have set for their co-workers. One entered Opportunity Village as a client, the other as a non-disabled employee. Yet both of them have shown that hard work and determination pay off, and that the only limit placed on a person at Opportunity Village is one they may place on themselves.

♥ ♥ ♥

The combined custodial contracts employ over 100 clients, and another fifteen or so non-disabled back fill workers, plus a staff of supervisory personnel. Before being employed under a custodial work service contract, a client receives vocational training at the West Oakey campus in a department set up just for that purpose. There is also some on-the-job training provided by supervisory staff.

Because JWOD pay rates are mandated by law, they are almost always higher that those paid on local government and private industry work contracts. For instance, as of early 2006, those clients working on a JWOD contract could earn as high as $10.72 an hour plus benefits, while those working under a local contract rarely go above $8.00 an hour. The advantage in this is that it offers the possibility of upward mobility for those clients who may wish to apply for a transfer from a local to a JWOD contract.

For all the success Opportunity Village has had building their work service contract business, and an outstanding reputation for the quality of its work, Elio Ramirez recalled one incident that shows how fate can make it all turn on the head of a pin.

New contracts in an unfamiliar building are always a challenge for clients. They are given pictorial maps and instructions, carefully color coded to show them where to go within the building to perform their work. One particular contract started well enough, and was sailing smoothly along. Then Ramirez got a call from the building, telling him that the first week had gone very well but that during the second week none of the cleaning had been done properly. He began to investigate.

One evening, as it turned out, the bus driver who delivers the clients to the workplace, in order to avoid parking in direct sunlight, decided to deliver the clients to the back of the building rather the front where they had normally been dropped off. Into the building through the back door walked the clients, and none of them knew where they were. They couldn't find the bathrooms they had normally cleaned, so in their confusion they did little.

Fortunately, Ramirez was able to turn the problem around; but it indicates how tenuous each contract can be without a lot of preparation, and just a tiny bit of luck.

Weinrich used the story to praise Ramirez, and to make a point about the importance of finding the right people for management at Opportunity Village. He said he had hired some managers who were good administrators, some who were good tradesmen, and some who were good at both. But, he said, before he found Ramirez, he hadn't found anyone who also had the heart necessary for the job. By heart, he was referring to someone who understands the clients, who respects their unique work ethic, and who understands how they think.

"We have two customers," Weinrich added. "We have the clients and their families, who are our customers, and we have these companies we clean for, who are also our customers. We have to understand them both."

♥ ♥ ♥

Work service contracts are not the only employment option open to Opportunity Village clients once they've completed their vocational training. They are also free to seek jobs outside of the organization, with a private employer in the community. There is a program available to assist those clients who are willing and able to take that big step. It's run by Dan Bickmore, Opportunity Village's director of community employment services.

"Opportunity Village is a person-based mission. We want to know what you [the client] want to do," Bickmore said. "If a person says, 'I want to detail cars,' we're going to see if that's possible. If he wants to push carts at Albertsons, or work at Radio Shack or Home Depot, we work to get that done for him."

Bickmore was born and raised in Chino, California. He moved to Las Vegas in the 1980s as an employee of the old Pacific Southwest Airlines; but after being transferred to Baltimore for eighteen months, he left the industry and went to work for the Riviera Hotel & Casino. Bickmore eventually became hotel manager, but he was ready for another for a career change.

His first wife's sister was born with severe disabilities, but Bickmore said he quickly learned to love and respect his sister-in-law, Theresa. Her disabilities, he said, "were just part of her personality; I got to know her as a whole person." So when he went to Opportunity Village in 2002 for a job inter-view, he said, "I saw people in the same situation as Theresa, so it was a nice, easy transition for me."

Bickmore's first job was in client intake services, as a computer operator, but after redesigning the organization's outmoded client intake computer program, he was offered a promotion to employment services manager, which led to his current position.

There are a number of client-centered programs under Bickmore's direction. One of the most important is placing clients in jobs throughout the community. The department will place approximately thirty to forty clients a year, but it is not a one shot task. Roughly six out of ten clients placed in a job will not work out, for a variety of reasons: scheduling problems, transportation or socialization issues are the top reasons.

"Every community job placement is prefaced by about 100 man hours of finding just the right

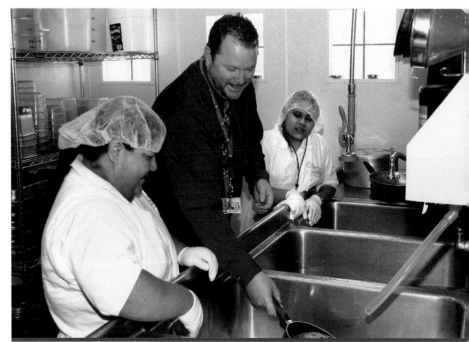

Director of community employment services, Dan Bickmore, offers instructions to Denise Retanna and Gloria Olivarrio in the state-of-the-art training kitchen.

employer, and the right employment situation," he said. "Getting somebody a job is the easy part . . . it's helping that person keep the job that's so difficult."

Bickmore's department spends most of its time shadowing its clients once they're placed in the new job. With higher functioning clients, only about five hours a month is required to actually observe them in the workplace, while lower functioning clients may require as much as forty hours a month. Bickmore related a recent story about one client who was placed in a large hotel/casino kitchen environment. "The employer demanded that we spend 160 hours with the client during the first month . . . if you do the math, that's virtually every single hour she worked." They did as the employer wanted, and the client has worked out well.

Once an Opportunity Village client has completed vocational training, a counseling session is held where everybody who has been involved with the client sits down to discuss the next step. Naturally, the client is part of the process, and ultimately it is the client's wish that dictates what happens next. He or she may elect to take a position in one of the organization's work service contracts, or if they are uncomfortable making any change, they may remain in one of the employment training centers. Many, however, will elect to take a job in the community and begin the long process of becoming independent. That process is called "inclusion" and it's the ultimate goal of Opportunity Village for every client it serves. However, since the Social Security payments that help most clients survive is a questionable long term issue, and many live with aging parents or caregivers, encouraging inclusion is a must.

Bickmore admitted, however, that many of the clients are not best served by seeking job independence outside the organization, without all its built-in support systems. But anyone who wants the chance will be given all the help and support Opportunity Village can provide for them.

Another program under Bickmore's direction is Community Outreach. This involves helping clients with problems that may occur outside of Opportunity Village's walls. "Let's say a client doesn't have a dentist, or he needs a lawyer, of he wants to know how he can get food stamps . . . we handle that," Bickmore said. He said his department also works with the public, answering questions they may have about vocational training, rehabilitation, housing for people with disabilities, and other related topics.

CHAPTER NINE

The Clients:
It's Not All About Work

The Amish, and their spiritual cousins the Mennonites, were originally invited to settle in Pennsylvania by William Penn himself way back in the late 1600s. Today, there are nearly twenty-five thousand Amish people in Lancaster County alone, the largest cluster of the sect in the country.

Many of their customs and religious values have changed little over the intervening centuries. The Amish eschew modern technology altogether, while the Mennonites are somewhat more accepting of mainstream American culture. One thing that has definitely changed, however, is today's high prevalence of certain rare, genetic-based diseases in both sects. Geneticists agree that the group's tendency to live in a restricted area and intermarry is the cause of these rare diseases.

The group's resultant physically and mentally handicapped members are referred to by the Amish as "God's special children," and are said to have been sent by God "to teach us how to love."

—Smithsonian *magazine, February, 2006*

Since its very earliest roots back in the early 1950s, Opportunity Village has been about one thing: serving citizens with intellectual disabilities and their families. First it was about the children, who were unable to attain the education that would allow them to make the most of their lives. Then, as our country gained a social awareness and came to embrace these children within the educational system, the priority shifted to providing services for adults with mental retardation.

Long hidden behind closed doors, and forced to live insular lives, adults with intellectual disabilities finally began to assimilate into the community-at-large after their schooling introduced them to life outside their four walls. Today, thanks to Opportunity Village, people with intellectual disabilities in Southern Nevada are able to train, work, earn a paycheck, and have rich social lives within a society that values those activities. Those whose disabilities limit their participation in activities still have a place within Opportunity Village. The programs are aptly named Project ENABLE and Project PRIDE.

All these men and women are the very core of Opportunity Village, its heart and soul, it's reason for being. They are people who today are able to make the best of what God has given them.

Despite their disabilities, these men and women are more like you and me than they are unlike us, yet they are as different from one another as you and I are from each other. They are not just severely disabled, they are Thomas and Patty and Mike and Carolyn and Shiela and Ann, and over three thousand other developmentally disabled people who are served by Opportunity Village's many and varied programs each year.

First and foremost, it is important to understand that people with intellectual disabilities *are not* emotionally retarded. They have the same feelings of joy and despair, of happiness and sadness, of contentment and apprehension, as the rest of us. More importantly, they have the same feelings of love and scorn, and of acceptance and rejection.

"You and I" is a program administered by the National Institute for People with Disabilities Network. Philip Levy, president of the organization, said in referring to people with severe disabilities, "People need to feel that they belong, that they're part of a community. That they're part of a relationship or relationships, and all of that contributes to a sense of self-esteem, to a sense of pride, to a sense of well-being."

People with intellectual disabilites are, first and foremost, just people. If there are areas in which "normal" people may outshine them, there are certainly areas in which the opposite is also true. Most people with these disabilities are guileless. Unlike the rest of us, who are constantly maneuvering to show ourselves in the best light, they do not hide behind a false façade. "Here I am," they seem to call out; "take me or leave me."

Likewise, they do not judge others by the color of their skin, the cut of their hair or the beauty of their features. Instead, they often seem to have a private peephole into another person's soul, and accept or reject that person based upon his innate virtues. I have been told by many clients, "I don't like mean people," and they seem to have a sixth sense about who the mean people are.

People with intellectual disabilities are often very emotional as well. Stripped of the artificial defenses the rest of us have constructed around ourselves, they are able to give free rein to their true feelings. They

Despite their disabilities, these men and women are more like you and me than they are unlike us . . .

wear their emotions on their sleeves. They value a genuine hug much more than a subtle wisecrack. If they like you, they tell you so. If not, they generally ignore you.

This is certainly not to say that they cannot be manipulative, but it is generally an innocent form of control they seek to exercise. At an informal parents' meeting, during one of Opportunity Village's monthly client dances, a number of parents shared pizza and wine, and a few stories, with me.

Paul and Silvia Sanchez of Las Vegas have two adult children who are clients of Opportunity Village. Their biological daughter Sandra, who loves art and crafts and music, is thirty-four (but for some reason, known only to her, claims to be fifty-four, according to Paul Sanchez.) Adopted son Kevin is thirty, and enjoys sports, especially wrestling. Both of their children also enjoy travel, according to Silvia Sanchez, and have traveled to Mexico City to visit family.

"They understand Spanish," Paul Sanchez said. "They don't speak it, but they understand it." Are there times when they pretend not to understand it, he is asked. The parents all laugh, enjoying a shared experience.

"Yes, they have selective hearing," he responded. "Kevin selects what he wants to understand. He looks at you as if to say, 'I don't understand,' but he understands."

When the 1990 Americans With Disabilities Act was passed, it was a landmark victory for the nation's citizens with intellectual disabilities, along with their counterparts with physical disabilities. The law prohibits discrimination against individuals with disabilities, and it is often described as the most sweeping nondiscrimination legislation since the 1964 Civil Rights Act. In areas of employment, public services, and public accommodations, the mentally retarded were finally given full citizenship. It was

long overdue. However, it still did not end the more indirect and insidious forms of discrimination that people with disabilities face.

Jason Kingsley and Mitchell Levitz are two extraordinary young men. Despite having Down syndrome, the two men wrote a book, *Count on Us: Growing Up With Down Syndrome*. Though the law now protects them from the worst forms of discrimination, it can't protect them from the mean people.

"People who are teasing me, they think they are cool," Kingsley wrote. "But they aren't. People who do the teasing don't know that I have feelings. My feelings get hurt."

That's one of the disadvantages of assimilating children with intellectual disabilities into society beginning with their earliest schooling. But, most would agree, it's a small price to pay for full citizenship. These special challenges will probably always be with them, but we can hope that some day, an enlightened public might finally get the message.

Opportunity Village is not a residential facility. The organization dabbled in adult housing for their clients back in the late 1960s, but when government housing assistance for the handicapped became available, the group eschewed that activity, although it is beginning to appear on the radar again. But Opportunity Village's 3,000 clients, just like the rest of the community, do not live in a vacuum. They may spend their days learning skills or working at one of the organization's facilities, or even within the community, but at quitting time, or weekends, they go home to lead the remainder of their lives like the rest of the citizenry.

There are three housing options available today for the citizens of Southern Nevada with disabilities. First, many live at home with their parents, siblings or other relatives. A second segment lives independently in the community, owning or renting an apartment or a house. They may live alone or, more frequently, with a friend. Among these are a few married couples that reside normally within the community.

The third living arrangement for people with disabilities are group homes. The state refers to these as "supportive living arrangements;" and through their local agency, the Desert Regional Center, or DRC, they do provide some funding for people living in group homes.

♥ ♥ ♥

One of those clients living at home with family is Thomas Dee Wilcox, sixty-one years old. A well groomed man of small stature with a shy smile and a quiet demeanor, Wilcox has thinning brown hair that is often covered with a favorite baseball cap. ("The Dodgers are my favorite," he beams.) As he gets to know you, Wilcox opens up, a common trait among people with mental retardation. As this metamorphosis occurs, a happy, genial man replaces the shy man with the downcast eyes of moments earlier. It's then you see the real Thomas Wilcox, a charming fellow with a quick smile and a ready hug for those he trusts.

Wilcox is unique in another way too. He is Opportunity Village's longest standing client, and the only living child of one of the CCARC founders still in the program.

Born to Carlyle and Jesma Wilcox in 1945, Thomas was a Down syndrome baby. His parents joined Al and Dessie Bailey and the other parents in founding CCARC, the forerunner of Opportunity Village, in 1954. Tommy, as he was known as a child, attended the Updike School and the Henderson based Carver Park School, the organization's first two attempts at establishing a private school for their children. When Clark County took over the operation of the Variety School for Handicapped Children and added space for these kids in 1957, Tommy became part of the first class.

On July 1, 1974, when Opportunity Village changed their focus to provide vocational training for adults, Tommy was one of the first participants. When asked how long he's worked at Opportunity Village, his brow furrows as he thinks. Finally, he replies, "It's been a long, long, long time."

Today, Wilcox lives with his nephew Wayne Leavitt and Leavitt's wife Nita in the house he has lived in for more than ten years. Leavitt, a woodworking teacher at Chaparral High School, is the son of Thomas's late brother-in-law, Max Leavitt. The Leavitts, the Wilcoxes and the Stewarts (the maternal family name of Thomas's sister Jesma "Peaches" Carter) is a large, extended family of Las Vegas pioneers.

In 2002, Wilcox's mother, also named Jesma, passed away at ninety-eight-years old, an emotional blow from which he has never fully recovered, according to his sister Peaches. Wilcox and his mom were very close, and worked together at the Church of Latter Day Saints one day a week for many years. Since his mother's death, Wilcox has become less communicative, but he still brightens up when a favorite subject arises in the conversation.

When he goes to work at Opportunity Village's West Oakey campus, Wilcox works in the mail center, collating contracts. But as a younger man, he worked at more active jobs. He spent many years working in the badge and button manufacturing department, and worked at cording headsets and coiling tubing. Like all clients, Wilcox is reevaluated on a regular basis to insure he is assigned a job that matches his shifting abilities and interests.

Regardless of the job he's employed in, Wilcox —like almost all Opportunity Village clients— absolutely loves to "go to the office." They love their work, the companionship of their friends, and the loving

Clockwise: *Thomas Wilcox helps with chores around his home. Thomas Wilcox enjoys a dance with his chief care-taker, Nita. Once an avid bowler and Special Olympics athlete, Thomas Wilcox still enjoys all his trophies. Thomas Wilcox stuffs pledge envelopes for his ward in the Church of Latter Day Saints, a task he's been at for decades.*

and helpful support of the staff and volunteers. Every day, Monday through Friday, Wilcox is picked up outside his front door at 7:15 AM by a Para-Transit bus and taken to work. "It's a very nice ride," he said. At 3:30 PM, he returns home. Every other Friday is a special day; when Wilcox comes home he brings his paycheck with him, and the sheer delight and sense of pride the paycheck represents simply cannot be overstated.

At sixty-one-years old, Wilcox is elderly for a person with Down syndrome. Few survive as long. His sister Peaches Carter and chief caregiver Nita Leavitt believe it's their large extended family, with so many people who truly love and respect him, that has kept Wilcox going. But there have been signs the past few years that time is creeping up on him. Hernia surgery curtailed his sports activities — for many years he was an avid bowler and Special Olympics participant — and cataract surgery was necessary to improve his sight. And, according to both ladies, his short-term memory is noticeably fading. In what seems to be an unfair case of double jeopardy, most Down syndrome adults will develop Alzheimer's disease, and do so much earlier than other people.

So although some of his favorite activities have had to be abandoned, Wilcox still has his likes and dislike. He collects baseball caps, and country western tapes, and enjoys helping Nita with basic household chores. He still does volunteer work for his ward in the LDS Church, stuffing pledge envelopes weekly. And he enjoys keeping trim. In the winter, he regularly used the treadmill machine in his bedroom, and swims frequently in the summertime. As for his dislikes, Wilcox is not a complainer. Like most people with this disability, he most dislikes an unexpected change in his schedule. Routine is very important.

Late in our visit, Wilcox defied all his ailments, and his age. With a twinkle in his eye, he grabbed Nita Leavitt's hand when a country western tune came on the radio. With the ease and grace of a much younger man, he whirled Leavitt around the floor in a joy-filled dance that had all of us enjoying the moment.

Thomas Dee Wilcox is an exceptional man. As the only person who has spanned the entire history of Opportunity Village and CCARC for more than fifty years, he is unique. He is truly one of God's special children.

Another longtime client of Opportunity Village living at home is Patty Forbes, a petite fifty-eight-year old woman with prematurely gray hair and a ready smile. She lives with her mom Pearl, who is also her best friend; her father passed away about four years ago. Pearl Forbes remembers those early days, in the 1950s, when there were few schooling options for children with mental retardation.

"I tried to sneak Patty into the school," she admits with a wry smile. "Later that day the teacher brought her home . . . she wasn't fooled. But she gave me the name of a woman she thought could help."

The person Pearl Forbes was referred to was one of the very early parents of the Clark County Association of Retarded Children; and she and her husband Ray quickly joined the nascent organization. When their daughter began school — it was CCARC's first school, the Updike School — there were only a few children attending.

Pearl Forbes recalls fondly the garage sales the early group held at Dessie Bailey's in order to raise money to support the school. Later, Patty Forbes attended and graduated from the Helen J. Stewart Special Education School.

Pearl Forbes also recalled a few early fashion shows they held with some of the donated clothing. The shows were held at the Variety School. "I had this one outfit I modeled . . . it was real fancy, and I had a long cigarette holder, and a fancy hat . . . it was such fun!"

Clockwise: *Patty Forbes enjoys drawing and water coloring when she is not at work. Patty Forbes loves her doll collection. Few remain, however, as recently, she donated the bulk of the collection to needy children. Patty and her mother Pearl Forbes often work side-by-side preparing meals.*

She had another fond recollection of an early concert in the 1960s. Wayne Newton was performing a special daytime show, and had invited a number of children with disabilities to attend as his guests. She had a group of twelve in her care. When the doors opened, the large crowd rushed in, immediately filling all the best seats.

Newton waved his invited guests to the front of the house, displaced many of the front row spectators, and sat the children down. Then he signed an autograph for each child.

"It was the most beautiful thing I've ever seen," Pearl Forbes remembered.

Today, Patty Forbes works in the Employment Training Center at the West Oakey Campus, where she does basic assembly and packaging work. Over the years, her mother said, Patty made a couple of attempts at joining the higher paid service contract workers, once in food service at Nellis and again in hotel guest services. But she was not able to perform at this more advanced level, nor was she happy at the job. "Patty works best in a sheltered workshop setting, so that's where we leave her," Pearl Forbes said.

Like most Opportunity Village clients, Patty Forbes takes great pleasure and pride in receiving her bi-weekly paycheck. "It's very, very important to her," her mother said. "When she asks how much she made, I just tell her, 'You made a whole bunch,' and she's as happy as she can be."

Pearl Forbes admitted that as she gets older, she worries about what will happen to her daughter when she's gone. But Patty's sister has already volunteered to step in when necessary, which relieves her mom's

mind. Pearl Forbes said she wanted to put her daughter in a group home years ago so she could learn to live more independently, and enjoy a fuller social life. But her husband wouldn't hear of it, so the family has always stayed together.

To this day, Pearl and Patty Forbes are still best friends. As they move busily around their small kitchen, working together to prepare for dinner . . . chatting idly about the day's happenings . . . you can see how they thrive together in the little home that is so obviously filled with love.

♥ ♥ ♥

Those Opportunity Village clients who do not have family in the area, or who are able, often opt to live independently in the community. They may live alone in a house or apartment, but more often live with a friend, significant other, or even a spouse. One of them is Mike Wilson.

Wilson, thirty-four years old, is a muscular, gregarious fellow with a shock of full, curly black hair. During the day, he works as a truck assistant at the Thrift Store on South Main Street. He alternates between working in the store's warehouse and going out into the community on one of the trucks to pick up donations, but in either case, the work is hard and physical. Wilson takes a bus to and from work every day, an hour's ride, but he says it doesn't bother him.

Wilson and his girlfriend Kim, a pretty, petite young lady of twenty-seven, live together in a small one bedroom apartment in the shadow of Black Mountain in the city of Henderson. The apartment is in a large complex of relatively new buildings with a central recreation room and pool. It's close to Kim's

Patty Forbes takes great pleasure and pride in receiving her bi-weekly paycheck.

job at a local Century movie theatre complex, a job she's held for more than seven years. Her parents live about fifteen minutes away.

Before living independently, Wilson lived in a group home in Las Vegas, but it wasn't a happy time for him. He's a high functioning person, and didn't like all the restrictive rules at the home. "I'm outgoing and I like to do my own thing," he said.

"Kim and I go to the movies together, and go out a lot; and at the group home I couldn't even go out without supervision."

The couple has lived in their apartment for just over seven months. They share the rent, and they share the work that comes with independent living. "I do all the housekeeping, and I do it every day," Kim said. "Mike fixes our meals."

"Yeah," he said with a wry smile, "but when I'm too tired I just put a frozen dinner in the oven."

Opportunity Village clients like Mike Wilson who live independently have a solid support team behind them, both to assist and to protect them. Wilson is assigned a caseworker from the Desert Regional Center (DRC) who checks in from time to time to make sure he's doing well. Wilson and Kim pay their own rent and living expenses, but if a situation ever arises when they run short of funds for something like food, his DRC caseworker helps out. "She helps us with our personal life," Wilson said.

In his work life, Wilson has a service coordinator from Opportunity Village, one of nine people filling those roles. Every client is represented by a service coordinator, who refer to themselves as advocates for their assigned clients. Of his service coordinator Wilson said, "If we've got complaints, we go to him and tell him about it. He's just there for all his clients."

Finally, Wilson and his girlfriend also have her parents who help out whenever necessary. Wilson lost both his parents not so long ago, so Kim's mom

and dad are like second parents to him. They do all the couple's bookkeeping and banking for them, and handle all their financial matters.

In addition to enjoying movies, the young couple also occasionally go to the Opportunity Village dances. He proudly showed a framed photograph of the couple in their formal attire when they attended the last Starlight Ball. They both enjoy sports too, and they're practicing for the state Special Olympics tryouts. "Kim got picked to go to nationals in track," Wilson said proudly, beaming at his girlfriend. "But she's not as fast as me," he added as an afterthought. "Yeah, but you're a guy," she said laughing. They obviously enjoy each other's company, and a lot of good natured banter goes on between the two.

As contented as they are with their life, Mike Wilson and Kim are thinking of moving to Branson, Missouri, with her parents when her dad retires in another six months. She has relatives there who will help them both get jobs, she said. Although you can tell Wilson is not completely convinced of the wisdom of the move, he too is tired of all the traffic and growth in Las Vegas. "I got my bike right there on the patio," he pointed. "But I don't even use it anymore. It's too dangerous. The cars, they use you for a target."

As I left their small, tidy apartment, I felt that this was a couple who be together for many, many years. They just seemed like a perfect fit for each other.

♥ ♥ ♥

The third housing option for people with intellectual disabilities in Southern Nevada is group homes.

Group homes serve all people with disabilities. In Clark County, group home housing capacity is not large enough to serve existing needs. The DRC, under whose auspices this housing falls, has stated unofficially that waiting time for a qualified person to find a spot can be up to a year and a half. Officially, DRC refused to comment for this book.

DRC supports group home programs for three different degrees of mental retardation. Supported Living Arrangement (SLA) supports individuals that have mastered several life skills and require assistance in only a few areas, such as banking, bill paying and other day-to-day financial matters. This program offers the most independence for residents. Group home operators staff these SLA houses only ten to twenty hours a week, with no sleepover staff required.

The next level is Transitional Supported Living Arrangement (TSLA.) It requires a little more support. Staff is in these homes twenty-four hours a day. They are what is referred to as sleep staff, so they are free to sleep through the night when the other residents have all retired.

The final group home level is Intensive Supported Living Arrangement (ISLA) that requires twenty-four hour awake staff. The individuals in these group homes have more behavioral and medical needs, and are usually more seriously disabled.

Up until recently, DRC also supported a fourth level of service, Intermediate Care Facilities, but they have dropped funding for that level of service, without official explanation.

DRC oversees group home operators in Clark County. Among them is New Vista Community, a not for profit operator of group homes that currently owns ten units in the county, and provides live-in staff services to another fifteen private homes that include residents with intellectual disabilities.

The northwest portion of Clark County has been one of the region's fastest growing quadrants for over a decade. Hundreds of new home developments have sprung up in that time, supported by retail development, schools, parks and other necessary services. At the farthest northern reaches of this area, fill-in development is still occurring. Brand new subdivisions share the landscape with yet to be developed parcels and small horse ranches.

Within this area, one of New Vista Community's ISLA homes is located. Situated in a typical suburban housing development — it appears to be only a couple of years old — it conjures up an image of a South Seas island with its catchy street names. The neighborhood is composed of large one and two story homes with red or gray tile roofs. Homes are painted in soothing pastel colors, with neatly manicured lawns. Just over the top of the houses you can see the dark, brooding shape of the Sheep Mountains, resembling an ancient island volcano. If you close your eyes you can almost imagine yourself in a Paul Gauguin painting. A white good humor truck moves slowly through the neighborhood with its bells gently tinkling, adding to the illusion.

In the midst of this idyllic setting is New Vista's one story home. Nothing in its outward appearance sets it apart from any of its neighbors. Three women with intellectual disabilities share the home, with one open bedroom awaiting a fourth resident. All of New Vista Community's homes are overseen by Archie McArthur, the organization's program director.

McArthur is a tall, handsome young man whose athletic build attests to his hobby as a semi-pro football player. He majored in civil engineering in college, and entered the field nearly a decade ago simply because he needed a job. Today, his resume includes working with troubled teens and men and women with developmental disabilities, and he is a certified trainer in behavior management. His calm, soothing demeanor belies both his career choice and his hobby, but it serves him well when dealing with the occasional neighbors who resent having a group home in their midst.

"Neighbors don't really understand our population," he said. "They often call these halfway houses, which they aren't. They want to get rid of us, so they often look for little things they can report to their homeowners' association."

McArthur said that most neighbors eventually come around when they discover that the group home residents rarely cause problems. As he pointed out, group homes are not halfway houses; they are regular homes with regular people who just require a little help with their daily living.

A tour of the home quickly fortifies that fact. It is very neat, very well maintained, and freshly painted. Each resident has her own bedroom and bath. The staff members that rotate through the twenty-four hour a day shift do not actually live on the premises. Each bedroom is individually decorated, and each resident has her own entertainment center with a TV, CD and video player, and even a personal computer if desired. In this ISLA home, staff has to work a little harder seeing that each resident keeps her own space clean and neat, but on our tour it certainly was.

The home is family oriented with everyone sitting down together for meals. Staff does the grocery shopping, and looks out for all the financial arrangements of the house: paying bills, collecting rent, overseeing maintenance, etc. Cleanup of the common areas is a group responsibility. The residents split the monthly rent, with funds they receive from Social Security. The State of Nevada makes up whatever shortfall may exist between Social Security benefits and basic living expenses. The money the residents earn through their jobs in the community, or in an employment training center, is their own, and staff

. . . group homes are not halfway houses; they are regular homes with regular people who just require a little help with their daily living.

assists them with their banking, or in management of a trust fund where their money may be held.

The house supervisor also provides recreational opportunities for the residents, assuring they enjoy a well rounded life.

"God has provided us with a really great staff," McArthur said proudly. He admitted that recruiting staff is the hardest part of his job, but added, "It's not really a difficult job, but you have to have a passion to work with handicapped people."

This particular group home is distinctive in another way. The three residents all came to the home directly from living at the DRC campus, a more institutionalized form of living, so it's their first step in transitioning into the community. The object of all group homes is to move each individual toward the maximum level of independence he or she may be capable of attaining. For some, they may never be able to advance past an ISLA home, but they still take pride in that level of independence.

A caseworker from DRC inspects each house on a regular basis to make sure everything is operating smoothly and the residents are being properly supervised.

In addition to eliminating financial support for Intermediate Care Facility housing in the community, DRC will soon be eliminating all their own onsite housing as well. When this happens, the current group home shortage in Clark County will only intensify, a problem Opportunity Village is watching carefully.

♥ ♥ ♥

Opportunity Village's nine service coordinators, referred to earlier, fulfill a vital role for their clients. Darren Hughes and Clark Adams are two of them.

Darren Hughes is a former professional football player, whose brief career was sidetracked by an injury. He initially came to Opportunity Village to visit a friend who worked at the agency, and discovered they were looking for volunteers on the employment training center floor because some staff members were unavoidably absent.

"I offered to volunteer that day," Hughes said. "At noon, they told me I could leave, but I didn't want to leave. They told me I could stay a little longer . . . then I came back the next day, and the next day; and they finally offered me a job." From that day Hughes worked his way up to his present position, a job he plans to keep for as long as he can.

Clark Adams, originally from Alabama, came to Las Vegas from Phoenix, where he had been employed by a social services program. He had family in Las Vegas who were involved with social work, so he became involved with group homes. Eventually he joined his brother-in-law at Opportunity Village, where he initially worked with some of the organization's clients with behavioral problems. "Two-to-ones they were called," Adams explained, those clients

Service coordinators Darren Hughes and Clark Adams assist Scott Ruggles, James Ruggles, and Patty Forbes as they learn a new task.

whose behavior disorders require a very high client to supervisor ratio. Eventually, like Hughes, Adams moved up to a job as a service coordinator.

Both men have now been with Opportunity Village for about five years.

"I believe the key ingredient to this position is patience," Adams said, "both with the client side and with the staff side . . . I believe the job title should be 'mediator.'" As the primary advocates for clients' rights, service coordinators are often the buffer between their clients and other staff members, parents, the ARC, group home operators, and any other individual or group with whom a client may have friction. "These folks don't know how to advocate for themselves," Hughes said, "so we have to advocate for them; we have to be their voice."

"You actually have to get on their level," he added. "You have to really understand your clients — really get to know them — before you can serve them."

The two men agreed that their clients have their rights abused on a daily basis, often by accident and often by well meaning people. They get overcharged at a store, or refused service because of their appearance or slurred speech. Even a client's family occasionally takes advantage of him by abusing his social security checks. The biggest problem for the service coordinator is to be alert to all the signs that might hint at an abuse of rights.

"There are things that they do, things that they say, that give you a clue," Hughes said. Again, it all comes down to getting to really know and understand each individual, the men agreed.

Service coordinators also create plans and goals for their clients, production goals and behavior goals. By carefully monitoring how well a client advances toward his goals they are able to detect if something may be off kilter in a client's life. "Non-verbal clues and body language are also important. These things tell us a lot," Adams added.

Like most service coordinators, Hughes and Adams are each responsible for sixty to sixty-five people, a significant caseload. They are able to stay on top of the caseload by constantly and informally meeting with their clients in the workplace on a daily basis. There is also a formal review every year for each person. A service coordinator, a caregiver or group home representative, and a DRC caseworker meet as a team to assess the client's progress and establish new goals and action plans. There is an action plan developed for work and one for home, and these become the road maps for the next twelve months. If there is a job change or other traumatic event in the client's life, additional team meetings are held to adjust the plans.

Both men and their wives attend all the big client dances and social affairs, and really enjoy seeing the other side of their clients at these events. "They exhibit a whole different side," Adams said, "and it's great to get to know them that way too."

The job of being an advocate for sixty people with intellectual disabilities does not sound like a glamour position. It's obviously not for everyone. But Darren Hughes and Clark Adams wouldn't have it any other way. Hughes had his brief fling with fame during his football days, but he insists it cannot compare with his present job. He also moved into management for four months at one point, but he missed the interaction with his clients, so he stepped back down. "Sometimes when I walk on the floor and my clients see me, they have a big smile on their face, and sometimes they're clapping . . . it makes me feel like a movie star . . . they make me feel so special," Hughes said.

Adams nodded his agreement. "In this job, I go home every day and I tell my wife — and she laughs — I tell her, 'I'm a hero every day,' and that keeps me going . . . I don't know how many people in the corporate life can say that."

Vicki Wesley, another service coordinator, advocates for the clients who work on the Nellis Air Force Base work service contract.

Wesley came to Las Vegas eighteen years ago, and entered social work as a group home worker. After doing that for seven years, she joined Opportunity Village. She is one of these people who has taken full advantage of the educational opportunities the organization makes available to its staff. "Next year," she said with justifiable pride, "I'll get my degree in social work."

Wesley echoed the words of many other staffers when she discussed the most difficult part of her job. "It's so hard to see people who have these desires . . . these dreams . . . and they can't get where they want to be because of their handicap."

Despite that, she is recharged daily by her work with her clients. "It's so rewarding to see people improving themselves," she said. "I absolutely love the job."

♥ ♥ ♥

The New Testament tells us, "Man shall not live by bread alone." Although many interpretations can be opined from St. Matthew's words, it's certainly clear that there is more to life than serving only its most elementary needs. Man — even when he has been disadvantaged by a mental handicap — needs more to flourish than simply a job.

From its earliest roots, Opportunity Village has realized that fact. As early as the mid 1960s, dance, music, and socialization had been added to the organization's programs. Today, leisure activities for its clients is a hallmark of the group.

The annual social calendar shows fourteen dances scheduled for the year, and there is something for everybody. Nine of the dances were scheduled for the West Oakey campus, and five for the Henderson campus, although every client is welcome at all of them. There was a Hawaiian luau dance, a western hoedown, a beach bash, and a fifties sock hop, to name only a few of the many themed nights.

My wife Cathy and I attended the Valentine's Dance at West Oakey. The long line outside that greeted us when we arrived should have given notice that this wasn't high tea; but still I hadn't expected what we experienced inside. I was amazed at the liveliness of the event. The huge gymnasium was festooned with colorful banners, and the lights were turned very low. A DJ played CDs at a deafening roar, songs that my sixty-nine-year old ears didn't recognize (nor want to.) I had been told that Opportunity Village's clients did not like loud noises; it upsets them. It was obvious, however, that this proclivity did not include the dances. Between the music and the happy chatter of more than 300 people, it was a din.

Heavy iron leg braces, and the helmets many wear in case of a fall, were not impediments to a rousing dance. Even wheelchair-bound clients were in the middle of the floor swaying their upper bodies to the music. Some of the most profoundly handicapped clients sat in their chairs at the perimeter of the gym watching the activity. It was impossible to gauge their reaction to what was going on all around them, but I don't doubt that they were having fun.

Briefly, I recalled my own high school dances. We were all so self-conscious about how we looked, and how our halting, unsure words would sound as we asked a cheerleader for a dance, that our minds blotted out everything around us. The few occasions when I was lucky enough to receive a smiling "yes" to the question, I was so self-absorbed at coming off "cool" that I don't even remember what the dance felt like. To be truthful, I don't remember a single high school dance fondly today.

Not so the clients of Opportunity Village. Unfettered by the need to be cool, they simply enjoyed the moment. What a revelation for me . . . too bad it came fifty years too late!

The highlight of the clients' social calendar is the Starlight Ball. Held every January, it's the big formal dinner dance and awards ceremony. Local hairdressers donate their time to make the ladies beautiful, and everybody is decked out in tuxedos and evening gowns. A sit down dinner, a lively dance, and an awards ceremony make the evening one to remember for all clients and staff.

♥ ♥ ♥

Bowling is one of the favorite leisure past times for Opportunity Village clients. Two twelve-week leagues are hosted by Special Olympics volunteers, and include a mixture of intellectually and physically disabled men and women. These are not officially sanctioned Special Olympics events. They are called recreational training leagues and are held simply for the fun of it.

Opportunity Village clients and staff enjoy a great Thanksgiving dinner at the Magical Forest.

Every participating bowler has an established handicap, and there are three separate divisions. The "Ramp Division" is composed of the lowest functioning teams. Many of these bowlers have profound disabilities, and in wheelchairs. In this division, a steeply inclined aluminum pipe ramp is positioned at the head of the bowling lane. An assistant or caregiver places the ball at the top of the ramp and aids the bowler in nudging the ball down the ramp, from which it gains enough speed to travel down the alley and strike the pins. The ramp can be repositioned to direct the second ball more accurately in order to pick up errant pins or even spares. Even a single pin knocked down becomes a major victory, and all the bowlers and fans clap and scream in delight.

"It isn't about the score," one cheering parent remarked. "It's just about being here, about participating, about being out in the world with your friends."

Despite the disabilities of the bowlers, there are some remarkably good scores noted on the Ramps Division score sheet. The high scoring games for the year are a 160 for the men and 133 for the women; high averages are 149 for the men and 96 for the women.

On this night, the Recreational Training League is occupying about two thirds of the Orleans Hotel and Casino's sixty-five lanes. That's about 130 bowlers; and a like number participate in the Tuesday evening league.

Richard Anderson and Rosie Scalf, enjoy one of the many Opportunity Village parties that are regularly scheduled.

The Division 2 bowlers are more functional, and much more vocal, in their support of their fellow athletes. A sweet looking woman with Down syndrome named Janie stepped to the line with her bright orange ball. With all her might, in a combination of a throw, a push, and a prayer, Janie launched the ball on its journey. It seemed to move at an agonizingly slow pace down the highly polished floor. The anticipation of the ball finally reaching the pins — if indeed it ever did — was palpable. But it finally arrived, at the far right hand corner of the neatly arranged triangle of pins, and amidst a sudden roar of approval, two pins surrendered to the ball and tumbled over. Janie was ecstatic!

Further down, the Division 1 bowlers were in full swing. These are the best of the best. A league high score of 194 for the men and 169 for the women attests to the talent at this level. Despite their advanced skills, they are as vocal as the others in expressing their enthusiasm at every ball.

My friends Mike Wilson and his girlfriend Kim are in this group. Marge Wilkes, a longtime Special Olympics volunteer, related a story about Wilson.

"He used to get so frustrated when he bowled," Marge said. "Then I told him he needed to use a heavier ball." Wilson is a big, muscular man, but Marge said he initially ignored her advice. "Finally, I found a heavier ball for him," she went on. "He raised his average by thirty pins; and he's been a happy bowler ever since."

Dan Bickmore, the director of community employment services, is also in charge of Opportunity Village's leisure and recreation program. He is very excited about the arts enrichment program, for which a 28,000 square foot facility will be built on the new southwest campus, a story detailed more fully in chapter thirteen. But if Bickmore has his way, these cultural programs will be started much sooner.

"We want to have it in place before the new facility is open," he said. He pointed out that all people with intellectual disabilities aren't employed, and Opportunity Village would like to be able to serve that segment of the community by " . . . giving them somewhere to go where they can let their creative juices flow." It's part of a plan to expand services past just meeting training and employment needs, Bickmore said.

About two years ago, Opportunity Village started a recreational program for its clients, but the program did not turn out as they had hoped, so it was cancelled. "We don't just want a respite program, a safe key program," Bickmore said. "We want to provide a true recreational experience; and we won't roll out the program again until it's truly a quality program."

Jean Perry, who heads up the operations side of the organization, echoed Bickmore's comments. The program had not met the recreational needs of its clients, she indicated, so it had become only a respite program for those participants that remained in it. Perry emphasized that if the new program correctly addresses recreational needs, the respite aspect — which simply means providing a needed break for caregivers — would automatically fall into place.

Bickmore gave credit to municipal recreation programs, and those sponsored by the YMCA and local churches. There are some excellent programs in the community for people with disabilities, and Bickmore said they don't want to just compete with others already doing the same thing.

One of the most popular recreational events for local members of the developmentally disabled community is not actually affiliated with Opportunity Village. It's the Special Olympics.

Special Olympics is sport in its truest sense, because the goal is not to win but to try. Open to all developmentally disabled adults and children over eight, the program was conceived by Eunice Kennedy Shriver in the early 1960s. The first games were actually held in 1968 in Chicago, and the program has never looked back.

Today, there are chapters of Special Olympics in every state in the nation, and more than 150 countries around the world. Nearly two million participants take part in the games each year. Supported exclusively by non-government funding, and run by a small army of volunteers, the events cover the entire spectrum of sport: aquatics and gymnastics, skiing and floor hockey, basketball and soccer, golf and bowling, and on and on, a total of twenty-six summer and winter sports. There is truly a place for everyone in Special Olympics.

Southern Nevada's involvement with the program has also made great strides. In 1975, there were only two athletes participating, both from Variety School. In 2005, nearly 2,000 athletes participated.

The Special Olympics oath opens every game. It says, "Let me win, but if I cannot win, let me be brave in the attempt." Athletes compete with those of their own age and level of ability, and everybody wins at least a ribbon. There are no losers in Special Olympics.

There's a heart-warming story about the Special Olympics that's been told and retold many times. Perhaps is true; perhaps it's become exaggerated in its retelling. Regardless, the spirit of the story is accurate even if the facts may have been glorified, so I've decided to repeat it one more time. If you know and love a person with an intellectual disability, you'll know the story rings true. It's called "The Candle."

A few years ago, during the Special Olympic Games, nine contestants, all with serious disabilities assembled at the starting line for the 100 yard dash.

At the gun, they all started out, not exactly in a dash, but with the relish to run the race to the finish and win. All, that is, except one little boy who stumbled on the asphalt, tumbled over a couple of times and began to cry.

The other eight heard the boy cry. They slowed down and looked back. Then they all turned around and went back . . . every one of them.

One girl with Down syndrome bent down and kissed him and said, "This will make it better."

Then all nine linked arms and walked together to the finish line.

Everyone in the stadium stood and the cheering went on for several minutes.

People who were there are still telling the story. Why? Because deep down we know this one thing:

What matters in life is more than winning for ourselves.

What matters in this life is helping others win, even if it means slowing down and changing our course.

A candle loses nothing by lighting another.

CHAPTER TEN

The Community:
It Takes A Village

We are all one. We cannot live for ourselves alone. Our lives are connected by a thousand invisible threads, and along these sympathetic fibers, our actions run as causes and return to us as results.

— *Herman Melville*

Herman Melville's words, penned over a century ago, still resonate today in Las Vegas, Nevada, perhaps the last place in America many people would expect to find so many charitable hearts living amidst the slot machines and glittering neon. But those people who live in the fastest growing metro market in America, know differently. Las Vegas is a very giving city, perhaps not in the conventional manner of most other cities, but in its own unique way.

Las Vegas branch executives at United Way, or at most other local chapters of leading national charitable organizations, would tell you contributions in their city fall below the national average.

The reasons for that fact, they would tell you, is that most Las Vegans are rootless; it is, and always has been, a transient market. People do not have that "sense of community" that comes with a stable, deeply entrenched population.

Those things are true. A brief look at the 2005 edition of *Las Vegas Perspective*, the area's premier annual demographic and statistical study of the market and its people, certainly back up that impression with some convincing figures:

> Population growth,
>   1994—2004:   +56.4 percent
> Percent of households with no children
>   under age 18:   69.1
> Percent of residents who were born
>   elsewhere: 96.8
> Percent of residents who have lived here less
>   than five years: 32.6
> Percent of households
>   that rent: 35.9

Each of these statistics point to a mobile population. Another group of questions from the annual survey of the population explored quality of life issues within the community, and they too back up the assertion that most Las Vegans are not as community oriented as in other cities.

To the statement, "I can recognize most of the people who live on my block," more than half of the survey respondents (51.6 percent) said that statement was "mostly false." To the statement, "Very few of my neighbors know me," 62 percent said it is "mostly true." And perhaps most telling of all, when asked to describe the sense of community with others on their block, only 10.4 percent said it was a strong sense of community.

While all of these factors contribute to a lower than average participation level with local charities, there is another side to charity, less obvious, more ethereal. When a story runs in the newspaper about a family whose home has burned down in the night, hundreds of Las Vegas companies and individuals immediately call with donations and offers of help. When a segment runs on television about an auto accident seriously injuring a local breadwinner, the station's phone lines immediately light up with generous offers of assistance for the family. And when a fatally ill child expresses a wish to see Disneyland once last time, the family is inundated with individual offers of help.

Most of these gifts and offers are made anonymously; they come from the heart, and no person or business is seeking recognition for their good deed. Perhaps this is the citizens' way of absolving a guilty conscious over their lack of traditional charitable giving. More likely, it simply comes from kind hearts that are more easily moved by an "in your face" tragedy, or the simple need of another human being in his time of despair.

In the case of Opportunity Village, however, all the conventional wisdom about Las Vegas' charitable giving goes out the window. The organization is dubbed "Las Vegas' Favorite Charity," a recognition that is not without serious backing. *The Las Vegas Review-Journal* has been conducting its "Best of Las Vegas" poll among readers and the population at large for twenty-five years. For the last ten consecutive years, and for a number of times before that, Opportunity Village has been selected "Best Community Organization."

Nobody is quite certain how this love affair between the organization and the community it serves began, nor can anyone explain its ongoing strength and commitment. Many people attribute it to one person, Linda Smith, the group's chief development officer, who for more than a quarter-century has been the high profile public face of Opportunity

Village in the Las Vegas community. Local business-man Bill Walters, one of the group's most generous benefactors, calls Smith "Las Vegas's Mother Theresa for people with intellectual disabilities."

Others attribute it to the Magical Forest and other annual fund raising events that have brought hundreds of thousands of Las Vegans face to face with the organization and the people it serves. And still others, taking a more practical approach, credit the fact that the organization has lifted the burden of caring for people with intellectual disabilities off the backs of taxpayers by being as self-sufficient as they are.

In the lobby of Opportunity Village's West Oakey campus is a large permanent display that recognizes the organization's financial donors. The donor board lists a number of giving categories, topped by a group called "Visionaries" who have contributed more than $1 million. Listed as Visionaries are ten individuals, corporations and government entities who have made those significant contributions. The next level of giving, "Platinum," honors contributors of $250,000 to $999,999, and another thirteen organizations and individuals are listed. An additional ten or more categories follow, and each proudly proclaims a number of the names of generous Las Vegans who believe in the causes of Opportunity Village.

The organization does enjoy an unequaled standing in the community. It is a position other not-for-profit organization professionals throughout Nevada, and indeed throughout the entire nation, would love to find themselves in.

♥ ♥ ♥

For the last nine consecutive years . . . Opportunity Village has been selected "Best Community Organization."

One of Opportunity Village's largest benefactors is the Walters family. Bill and Susan Walters came to Las Vegas from Louisville, Kentucky, in 1982 with their two sons Scott and Derin. Bill also has a daughter, Tonia, from an earlier marriage who lives in Las Vegas. The Walters' son Scott has an intellectual disability, but through hard work and help, he now lives a happy and fulfilled life back in his hometown of Louisville.

William T. "Bill" Walters is a trim, early sixty-ish man with silver hair and a handsome face that belies his age. His business card says he is the Chairman and Chief Executive Officer of Walters Golf, his own firm that owns and operates four successful golf courses in the city. But when asked his occupation, Walters is much more forthcoming. "I came here to pursue a career as a professional gambler," he admits. "The things I wanted to do from a career standpoint . . . Las Vegas allows me to pursue a career in gambling in a legal, lawful manner." Taking a broader perspective, Walters said, "I consider myself a professional risk taker."

Walters is also a very newsworthy person in the Southern Nevada community. Perhaps "controversial" would be a better word, a label he does not deny. "When you're a risk taker, it goes with the territory," he smiled.

At Opportunity Village, and among the city's mentally handicapped population and their advocates, Bill Walters has another name: hero. The commitment to the cause of people with intellectual disabilities by Bill and Susan Walters is beyond question. The Opportunity Village facility in Henderson, a community immediately southeast of Las Vegas, is aptly named the Walters Family Campus. The campus opened in 2000 to serve the people in that portion of Clark County, and was largely funded by a capital contribution from the Walters family.

One of Walter's most cherished possessions is a large color photograph that hangs proudly in his office. In it, he and Susan beam at the camera, standing beside a magnificent carousel the family donated, and still financially maintain, for the annual Magical Forest event. On the matting all around the picture are the "thank you" signatures of every client at Opportunity Village. From neatly printed names to scrawls that are barely decipherable, each name reminds the Walters of a separate story of the challenges faced and overcome by their friends at Opportunity Village.

How the group obtained the carousel is a story in itself, and its very typical of the way things happen when Bill Walters decides to get something done.

About four years ago, a local shopping mall offered to donate its carousel to Opportunity Village. Everyone became excited about what the beautiful merry-go-round would mean to the annual Christmas

Opportunity Village's magnificent carousel is one of the favorite attractions at the Magical Forest each Christmas.

event. However, at the last minute the mall withdrew its offer and sold the carousel to another mall in Minnesota. When Walters heard about it, he never hesitated. "Forget them; we'll get our own carousel," he thundered, and in typical Walters fashion, he did just that.

Amusement park giant Chance Industries of Wichita, Kansas, owns the molds and manufacturing rights to the intricately carved antique carousel reproductions that many of us grew up with. Working through Clown World in Henderson, Opportunity Village ordered one, modified to accommodate wheelchairs. An anonymous donor chipped in some money to help out, and with the Walters family fronting most of the cost, the carousel was purchased. Today, it is not only one of the featured attractions at the annual Magical Forest event, it is also used a couple of times each week during warmer months for clients to enjoy during their lunch break.

The Walters not only give money, they also give their time. Bill was a board member for many years, and is still considered one of the chief go-to guys when something needs to be accomplished. He and Susan can also be found at many fundraising events. At the annual Magical Forest, they sell tickets, serve food, and help children get on and off the small train which tours the Christmas fantasyland.

In typical fashion, Bill Walters minces no words when asked what his emotional connection is to the Opportunity Village clients he calls friends. "These people are my role models," he says. "To put it in gambler's terms, they got the hand that God dealt them . . . and they don't complain about it. They are the bravest, proudest, hardest working people I've ever known."

"They want to work, they want to contribute to society. It's difficult to understand how they endure all their challenges and still they are always in a great mood . . . always positive," he said.

"How do you thank someone who is so generous of heart," Linda Smith says of the Walters Family. "From their first association with Opportunity Village . . . the Walters have heeded the call of our valley's most vulnerable citizens. They truly define what it means to give back to those in need," she said.

Not all of Opportunity Village's supporters come from the ranks of those who have a close relative with a disability. Many of them are simply people with big hearts who are drawn to the plight of their fellow man.

Everything about Brian Janis says "laid back." His hair hangs down to his collar, and he is much more comfortable in jeans and a sweatshirt than in the slacks and tie that predominate in the industry where most of his clients reside. Even his business, Phototechnik International, is laid back, spread over three equipment filled rooms in the lower floor of his attractive two story suburban home. "I use to have a studio," Janis said, "but I'm much more comfortable working here at home." His staff heartily agrees.

Even his wife doesn't seem to mind all the comings and goings. "She's from a big family where eight or ten people lived in the house, so she's used to the activity," Janis said. "Without it, she gets bored."

But when Janis prepares for a professional photo shoot, or when he discusses the reason he has provided more than twenty years of *pro bono* photography work for Opportunity Village, the casual demeanor disappears and is replaced by serious and thoughtful reflection. He is very serious about his work, and he is very serious about Opportunity Village.

Janis came to Las Vegas from New Jersey in 1983, following college. He immediately went to work as director of photography for Greyhound Exposition

Services, Las Vegas' largest convention and exhibition services provider. After spending two years in that job, he started his own business with a friend, then eventually started Phototechnik International on his own. On the firm's web site, you can still get an inkling of the informal way he prefers to work: his self appointed title is "President and Chief Photodude."

Janis was introduced to Opportunity Village more than two decades ago while he was doing some work for a local advertising agency. The agency was doing a job for Opportunity Village, and asked Janis if he'd volunteer some time to shoot pictures. He agreed. The photos he was asked to shoot had to with the 1985 Concert of Love. That year's guest artist, Tony Orlando, was visiting the employment training center, and Janis followed him around with his camera.

"The clients were all excited to see Tony," Janis recalled. "They all knew who he was."

"I guess Tony is a hugger. As we went through, he would stop and hug the clients, and they got all excited and turned around and wanted to hug somebody else. I was right there, so I probably got a dozen hugs that day from the clients, and after that, I was hooked," he smiled, recalling the day.

Janis was asked to shoot the actual concert, and he readily agreed. It's been a real love affair between Brian Janis, Chief Photodude, and Opportunity Village's hundreds of clients ever since.

When a small business adopts a non-profit cause to support — Janis actually supports three with free photography — it's much different than when a large firm with hundreds of employees donates in-kind services. That statement certainly isn't intended to denigrate the support donated by the larger employers of Las Vegas; it is vital to Opportunity Village's success. But there is very little elasticity in the workday for a staff of four, and when one of their number spends hours in the field on a *pro bono* job, somebody else has

to pick up the slack or the bread and butter business must be put on hold.

But most standards, Phototechnik is a small business. But in the world of photography, where freelancers still dominate, it is considered a substantial firm. There are four fulltime employees, and six to eight freelance photographers who are constantly on call as jobs arise.

Most of the firm's business today is done with conventions, corporate meetings, entertainment events, and hotel/casinos. It's a hard job that requires lots of night work. Still, there always seems to be time when Opportunity Village calls for a favor.

"They have a lot of events," Janis said, "and they want to capture a visual history of each event. So we're constantly on call for them." Asked what keeps his interest after all these years, Janis admits it's still the clients. "I enjoy working with the marketing staff, but it's still about the clients. I just feel good about myself at the end of a shoot."

Today, Opportunity Village has little problem finding assistance. It wasn't always that way. In the earlier days, before people became more enlightened, there weren't as many organizations ready to step in to answer the call. But there were exceptions, and many were the community's earliest women's organizations.

Today, women are among the ranks of Rotarians and Chambers of Commerce, Elks Clubs and Variety Club and Veterans of Foreign Wars. But it was not always so. Like people with disabilities themselves, there was a time — not so very long ago — when women were expected to "know their place," and their place was not as part of an exclusive men's club. The women had their own organizations. Many of those clubs were independent, but many were women's auxiliaries of the same clubs that would not admit them as members.

According to Joan Whitely, in her book *Young Las Vegas*, the Mesquite Club for Women was Las Vegas' first women's organization. Started in 1911, it is still operating today. One of its founding members was Helen J. Stewart, Las Vegas pioneer and ex-rancher whose roots in the area pre-date the 1905 founding of the city itself. The club's initial stated purpose was "dedicated to the enrichment of everyday life in the emerging city of Las Vegas."

The earliest recorded history of community service to all people with disabilities Las Vegas is studded with mentions of the Mesquite Club. They sponsored a number of events during the early 1950s where the proceeds were dedicated to the cause of the community's handicapped members. When there was nobody else there, there was the Mesquite Club.

Today, the Mesquite Club no longer actively supports Opportunity Village. As other organizations came along to fill that role, Mesquite Club members moved on to other, equally worthy causes within the

42 Las Vegas Review-Journal   Sunday, May 19, 1963

planned benefit set

HONOREE AND SPONSORS

At top right is Mrs. Elbert (Dessie) Bailey, president of the Clark County Association for Retarded Children, who will be the honored guest at a benefit party sponsored by the sustaining members of Service League on May 25. Mrs. Robert O. Cannon, left, and Mrs. David Boles, center, are co-chairman of the party on behalf of Service League. All profits from the party will be used toward a workshop and training center for the retarded. The fete will be a "Hoedown for Dessie." And should party guests arrive at the Walter Johnson home, 410 Rancho Road, without proper headgear for the Hoedown, they will find the super-salesman team of Allen and Down ready to serve them. Bottom picture, left to right, Mrs. James H. Down, Mrs. Harry Allen, Down, and Allen. *Review-Journal Photos*

A 1963 news article tells how the Service League (now the Junior League) honored CCARC founder Dessie Bailey.

community that they still serve with dedication and distinction to this day, nearly 100 years after their founding.

In 1946 another women's organization sprang up with an equally lofty calling of supporting the community. The Service League was founded by seven prominent local women. They invited seventeen other young women to join them in their good works. By 2005, the Service League — renamed the Junior League of Las Vegas in 1971 — had contributed more than $1,350,000 and thousands of hours of volunteer time to the community.

Still highly visible today in the community, the Junior League began its service to the mentally handicapped in 1963 with the establishment of the Nursery School for Retarded Children. Following the group's normal procedure, the school was turned over to the Clark County School District to operate once it was functioning smoothly.

The Junior League's $5,000 contribution in 1965 helped build the first Opportunity Center, Opportunity Village's first permanent employment training center. Junior League continued to support Opportunity Village's early years with fashion shows, raffles and other fundraising events that helped the organization gain the early traction that has served it so well to the present day.

The Women's Auxiliary to Variety Club Tent 39 was officially launched in 1956, and was also an early supporter of the area's children with disabilities.

The founding members of the group, whose stated goal was to support Variety Club's charitable endeavors, was a who's who of the wives of early Las Vegas gaming and community giants: Mrs. Ben Goffstein, Mrs. Wilbur Clark, Mrs. Ernest Cragin, Mrs. Jacob Kosloff, and Mrs. Joe Rosenberg. A few of the Auxiliary members' husbands, as well as a few other early members of the local Variety Club, were reputed to be mob connected, but this was, after all, Las Vegas in the early 1950s.

Today, the group no longer exists, as women are welcome members in Variety, the Children's Charity.

Last, but by no means least, was Opportunity Village's own women's auxiliary, the Vanguards, organized in 1971.

Fledia Sardelli is a beautiful woman, now nestled comfortably somewhere in her sixties. Her trim figure is a reflection to this day of the dancer/choreographer she was in Texas in her youth. She and husband Nelson, a longtime singer/actor/entertainer, have lived in Las Vegas for nearly forty years.

By the early 1970s, Sardelli's mom had joined the couple, helping to care for their three children. It was her mother, Sardelli admitted, who pushed her out the front door and told her to find something meaningful to do with her spare time. Her husband had taken an early interest in promoting the welfare of children with intellectual disabilities, and had even staged a fundraiser he called Star Shine in Puerto Rico to benefit the cause, so it was only natural that Sardelli decided to get behind that cause in Las Vegas.

"I looked in the phone book," Sardelli said, "and I found Opportunity Village, and I went down to volunteer." The next day, she got a phone call from executive director Ted Johnson, who had come on board four years earlier and laid the groundwork for what Opportunity Village would eventually become. Johnson and Toni Front, wife of a Sahara Hotel executive, had discussed starting a women's auxiliary, and Johnson asked Sardelli to head up the effort.

"I had never done anything like this," she admitted, smiling warmly at the recollection. "But Ted had a lot of ideas to get us started. He said, 'Stay small — only twenty-five or so members. If it gets any bigger, people begin to bicker and it stops being an effective working club.'"

Toni Front decided to host a tea and invited some friends, and they invited their friends, and when the day came, almost magically, twenty-five women showed up. The Vanguard Club was officially launched with Fledia Sardelli as the first president She is amazed to this day at how perfectly the group meshed together. "Every single one was a hardworking, caring person . . . it was a godsend," she said, adding that each women came with good ideas, a great mix of different talents, and the desire to see the mission through.

It took no time at all for the Vanguards to begin their legacy of service to Opportunity Village. At the first meeting, one woman suggested that to raise funds for the thrift shop, Opportunity Village's most important revenue producer, perhaps they could stage a fashion show featuring — believe it or not — second-hand clothing. The suggestion was immediately approved, and preparations began.

Colleen Schroeder, a member of the group, was the fashion coordinator at The Broadway Department Store, and she assumed control of the event. "She was a miracle worker," Sardelli beamed. "She put together the most clever, creative, entertaining fashion show imaginable, all with used clothing; and it was a big success." The event was held at the Sahara Hotel, and was so popular that it was repeated for many years.

By the late 1970s, the hand-me-down clothing had been supplemented with brand new fashions donated by area clothing stores, and sold at next-to-nothing prices in the thrift store. A 1978 article in the **Las Vegas Review-Journal** reported, "New and near-new clothing with brand name labels will carry price tags of $3 to $20. Fashions valued at $100 and more will average $25. Only a few gowns will sell for more, but they will be worth it."

In addition to the fashion shows, the Vanguards sponsored car washes, bake sales, and published a "Cookbook of the Stars."

Martine Roy (from left,) Leslie Roy, Colleen Schroeder and Dottie Saligoe prepare to take the runway for the 1973 Vanguard Club's annual fashion show.

Eventually they even resurrected Nelson Sardelli's Star Shine gala for three years. The Sahara donated use of a huge ballroom, and attendees mingled with celebrities and local bigwigs. Harking back to the Variety Club's Night of Stars, a number of Strip entertainers, including Nelson Sardelli, entertained at the events.

One of the biggest attractions was an idea from which the Star Shine name was taken. Big name stars, and national and local celebs, shined shoes for the guests at laughingly inflated prices. One piece of ephemera in Fledia Sardelli's scrapbook, a small ticket, proclaims, "Ron Lurie [mayor of Las Vegas at the time] will shine Al Levy's shoes for $25."

"It was such fun," Sardelli remembers. "Political enemies bid against each other to see who would have to shine who's shoes."

Just as Ted Johnson had initially warned, after about ten years of spectacular service to Opportunity Village, the Vanguard Club grew too large, and its effectiveness waned. Eventually, the club disbanded. But none of that could diminish the fact that during its heyday, the Vanguard Club had been a huge success.

❤ ❤ ❤

Most people who donate their time or resources to Opportunity Village report that they get back much more than they give. They are referring, of course, to that special feeling a person has when he or she has done something good for another person. It's an inner glow, kind of like a hug for your soul, that's unmatched by any other human feeling.

Members of the Southern Nevada chapter of the National Railway Historical Society (NRHS) know that feeling well, since they have been volunteering their time, expertise and money to Opportunity Village for over a decade. But for them, there is a

bonus in their volunteer efforts: they get to do what they love best, which is working on trains.

A couple of years after Opportunity Village started their hugely successful Magical Forest holiday event in the early 1990s (see chapter eleven) they had a miniature railroad installed that toured the property. But in 1996, the railroad's owner reclaimed his train and tracks, and "Chief Elf" Linda Smith — the person in charge of such things — knew she had to find a replacement. She managed to find an old beat up, rusted hulk of an amusement park train in California, and she purchased it, with absolutely no idea what she was going to do next.

To the Chief Elf's good fortune, the Great American Train Show happened to be staging their annual show at Cashman Field that year; and Smith, the Chief Elf, went calling. NRHS's local chapter had set up a booth to recruit new members, and Smith stopped by and chatted with Tony Bond, who was manning the booth that day.

Bond grew up as an Army brat, and became fascinated with steam locomotives while living in Germany. He'd spend hours shooting black and white snapshots as the trains thundered by. But like most young men, he put his interest aside as he grew up, went to college and entered the workplace in television production. Years later, perhaps by fate, he received an assignment to shoot some footage of the Nevada Northern Railway in Ely, Nevada, and his passion was immediately rekindled.

Bond asked how he could become involved, and was told, "You come up here, plan to get your hands dirty, plan to learn railroading from the ground up, and we'll help you get there." Today, Bond is still involved with the Nevada Northern Railway in Ely, and with the Southern Nevada Railway in Boulder City. He's also a Federal Railroad Administration certified steam engineer and diesel engineer.

Bond had already done a few *pro bono* video production jobs for Opportunity Village before he and Smith met that day at the Great American Train Show, but when she laid out her current problem for him, he was immediately hooked. He presented Smith's problem to the NRHS membership, and they got on board. "They were complaining that all we ever did was watch videos, drink tea, and eat cookies," Bond recalled, "so the idea of actually working on a real, live train was exciting."

There was only one problem: it was already September, and the Chief Elf wanted her old hulk of a train up and operating by late November for Magical Forest. "The first problem with it," Bond remembered, "was that it was an odd eighteen-inch gauge train, and most amusement trains were fifteen or sixteen inch gauge." Worse yet, he recalled, it was a rust bucket.

"We had to tear the train down to absolutely nothing," he said. "We stripped it all the way down to its bearings . . . axels that had to be re-turned . . . wheels that had to be repaired . . . it was a mammoth job." But the members loved it. They pitched in and spent every available hour working on the train, and laying the new tracks, and like good railroad men for nearly two centuries, they made their deadline and the train was ready when the Magical Forest opened in 1996.

Today, Opportunity Village has two trains in order to meet demand, the older *City of Las Vegas* and the newer *City of Henderson.* The latter, a standard sixteen inch gauge model, had to be adapted to fit the odd eighteen-inch track. Both trains have been adapted to carry those in wheelchairs. The two trains have a fine depot, donated by the gaming giant Boyd Gaming Corporation, and a miniature tunnel, built by Marnell Corrao Associates. But the figure-eight track layout, all the rolling stock, and the computer controlled automatic switching system, were built and are maintained by NRHS members. The tunnel doubles as the train garage and workshop.

In 2005 Tony Bond, who is semi-retired after selling his TV and video production company, gave up his official title as Chief Operating Officer of the Opportunity Village Railroad to a fellow NRHS member. However, he remains as active as ever. Bond explained that it takes 10 people each night during Magical Forest to operate the railroad. During the year there are fifty to sixty NRHS volunteers who work at the facility maintaining the tracks and equipment. They also service and maintain Opportunity Village's magnificent carousel.

Working on the railroad is a labor of love for NRHS's members, but Bond is quick to point out that there is another, more important reason the group has remained so dedicated to the Opportunity Village Railroad. "The bottom line is, we're helping Opportunity Village because were making money for them to support their programs," he said proudly.

Sometimes, when the crew is at work, Bond said, clients will stop by and shout, "Hey, railroad man! Hey, railroad man!" with wide grins and hearty waves. "Then you realize, man, this is cool . . . you fall in love with it," he admitted.

"It's been one of the richest rewards of my life."

Before there was an Opportunity Village, even before there was a Clark County Association for Retarded Children, there was a group of parents trying to find a way for their children to get schooled. Also in the late 1940s and early 1950s, when Las Vegas was little more than a dot on the map, there were hotels and casinos. There weren't too many of them then, and they were not the billion dollar, world class resorts we're familiar with today, but still, they were there.

This beat-up, rusted hulk of an amusement park train eventually became a gleaming beauty thanks to the work of the Las Vegas chapter of the National Historical Railway Society.

These were the very first businesses to stand up and be counted when the parents of the dusty town's mentally handicapped children began looking for help. The story of these businesses, and the Variety Club they founded in order to support the community's needs, is detailed in chapter eleven, "The Big Event," so we won't repeat it here. But the tradition of community support from the hotel and gaming industry is long, and its roots go deep.

Today, there are very few gaming establishments in Southern Nevada, or their employees, that have not stepped up to help Opportunity Village when the call went out.

One such company is Station Casinos.

In 1976, Frank Fertitta Jr. opened a small 5,000 square foot entertainment venue designed specifically for Las Vegas locals at the corner of Sahara Avenue and Industrial Road. He called it simply The Casino. Although Fertitta's small joint had only about 100 slot machines and a snack bar, locals immediately

took to it. Over the next few years, he expanded the property a number of times, and changed its name to Bingo Palace. In the early 1980s he changed the name again, this time to Palace Station.

Today, Station Casinos, Inc., is run by Frank Fertitta's two sons, and it is the market's largest gaming company geared toward locals. Ten major hotel/casinos operate under the Station banner, along with a handful of smaller neighborhood casinos. The company also has four major parcels of land in Las Vegas and two in Reno that it plans to develop over the next decade.

More than 14,000 employees — called team members — work for the company, which has twice been named one of *Fortune Magazine's* "100 Best Companies to Work For."

Scott Nielson is Station Casinos' Executive Vice President and Chief Development Officer. He has also been a member of Opportunity Village Foundation's board of directors for the past fourteen years, and has served a term as Chairperson of that group. Originally from Salt Lake City, Utah, Nielson has resided in Las Vegas for twenty-five years. An attorney, he was hired as Station Casinos' general counsel in 1991, before moving to his present position.

"Station was involved with Opportunity Village in various ways prior to my joining them in 1991," Nielson said. "The Fertitta family has always helped the organization in one way or another." He admits, however, that the company's involvement has increased since he gained his seat on the Opportunity Village board.

"My youngest brother has disabilities, and so I certainly understood the challenges he faced, and my mother faced as well. That's why Opportunity Village has always been near and dear to my heart," Nielson said.

Fourteen years ago, when Opportunity Village inaugurated it's very successful Jeans to Jewels fundraiser, Station Casinos volunteered to provide all the food for the event. Now, nearly 10,000 great BBQ dinners with all the trimmings later, they are still cooking up great food for the 600 to 800 guests who attend each year.

"It's a big undertaking," Nielson admitted, "and it gets bigger every year. But it's a lot of fun . . . it's a great event, and everybody dresses up in jeans and cowboy hats and just has a good time."

The company and its team members are also involved in the annual Magical Forest. They provide all the staffing for one evening each year, anywhere from fifty to 100 people depending upon the night. Nielson explained that the company works hard at providing its team members with positive exposure to Opportunity Village and its clients so they will all be working toward the same goal.

"We have our Christmas parties down there too, at Magical Forest, so all our team members get a chance to go through it. We pay for it, of course, but it gets our team members familiar with the mission."

Station Casinos also has a very novel and generous program they call "Caring for our Community." Every year nine non-profit charities are selected from the community. Each group receives a $50,000 donation and a thirty day television and newspaper aware-

Station Casinos has been donating all the delicious food for the annual Jeans to Jewels fundraiser since its inception more than a decade ago.

Guests at Jeans to Jewels hoedown love the BBQ buffet supplied by Stations Casinos.

ness campaign to spotlight the charity's mission and needs. Opportunity Village has been selected twice over the years as a recipient of the program. Station Casinos also supports a number of other Opportunity Village fundraising events with cash and services.

Finally, the company has also hired many Opportunity Village clients over the years for house-keeping and culinary work. Many of these people are still on the payroll, proud to be team members.

Asked why he believes the community has sup-ported Opportunity Village so passionately over the years, Nielson has a strong opinion on the subject. "It's a well run organization . . . they know what they're doing, and people appreciate that," he said. "And when you see the good work they're doing with the clients and their families, that touches people on an emotional level . . . it makes them want to help."

♥ ♥ ♥

Many men and women in the community donate their hard earned dollars to Opportunity Village. Others generously donate their time, working along-side the clients in one of the organization's many rev-enue producing departments, or at one of the many fundraising events. Still others, like the railroad enthusiasts, use their unique expertise and talents to assist in special problem areas. And finally, many con-tribute much needed supplies and equipment to help the organization achieve their goals. Such is the case with Desert Buick GMC.

Larry Carter is a taciturn man, not given to wild extravagances of speech or a lot of wasted words. But you can instantly tell that he's a man who is comfort-able in his own skin, and has pride in the things he's accomplished through a lifetime of hard work.

Carter was born and raised on a farm in Michigan, and after school, he found his way to General Motors. But being part of a huge multinational corporation wasn't the best fit for him. "I grew up on a farm, and I just wasn't use to being in a three-piece suit," he smiled. "I wanted to get out of that world." So in 1971 when GM offered him a GMC truck franchise in Las Vegas, he jumped at the chance. The company was willing to hold the franchise for him for two years while he found a financial backer, and in 1973 he arrived in Las Vegas the proud owner of a truck store.

His first GMC store was on West Tropicana, then only a two lane road, at the I-15 freeway. "We were in the middle of nowhere," he recalled. A few years later, Carter opened a second store on East Sahara, then known as "auto row," and in 1991 added the Buick franchise and moved to the store's present location on West Sahara.

In 1997 Carter sold his dealerships to AutoNation, then part of Republic Industries, which was fast turn-ing the retail auto industry from a sole ownership business into a vast nationwide dealership conglomer-ate. Today, AutoNation owns nearly 300 retail auto locations across the country. In 2000, the Southern Nevada subsidiary was renamed Desert Automotive Group, and today includes twelve Clark County loca-tions representing sixteen new car franchises.

Carter was appointed Las Vegas market president for the entire group, a position he held until his retire-ment in December 2004.

In the mid 1980s, long before the AutoNation days, Carter met Linda Smith. She gave him a rundown on Opportunity Village, and he recalled thinking, Finally, here's a charity that's doing everything pos-sible to be self supporting. That appealed to the busi-nessman in him, and when Smith called some months later looking for help, Carter donated two mini-pick-ups to the organization.

In the twenty plus years since, Carter estimates he's donated close to a dozen trucks to the cause. He's quick to point out that Opportunity Village hasn't abused his charitable spirit. "More times that not," he said, "we've called them and asked, 'What do you need?'" The gifts have included pickups and mini-pickups, vans and cars, even a large box truck used to pick up donations for the thrift store.

Larry Carter's softer side comes out when he describes why he's been so generous to Opportunity Village. "I can't personally help the clients," he said. "But one thing I can do is support them financially." In addition to the donated trucks, Carter also makes financial contributions, both personally and through his businesses, something he has continued to do since his retirement. Carter has also left a legacy for service that will help Opportunity Village long into the future. Under his direction, the entire Desert Automotive Group has continued its support, includ-

ing providing all the volunteer staffing for one night of the Magical Forest, nearly one hundred people.

As a man of few words, Carter sums up his feeling about Opportunity Village simply: "It's my favorite charity in Las Vegas."

Attempting to create a roster of all those Southern Nevada individuals, businesses and organizations that have supported Opportunity Village's programs over the past fifty-three years would be impossible. The list would simply be too long. It would include average citizens, the city's rich and powerful, and the political elite. It would include dozens of different trade unions, fraternal organizations and small businesses. It would include churches, hobby clubs, and multinational corporations. Our roster would of

A common sight throughout the community is the big Opportunity Village donation pickup truck, donated by Desert GMC.

course include many schools, professional organizations, and religious groups, and seniors' organizations, veterans' organizations and volunteer services. Social clubs and neighborhood organizations can't be forgotten, nor can cultural groups, government agencies and self-help groups.

Being more specific, the list would include Rotarians, Elks and Kiwanians, chefs, clowns, entertainers and entrepreneurs. Also included would be the Junior League, food and beverage directors, numerous advertising agencies, Boy Scouts and Girl Scouts, Jaycees and Jaycee-ettes, fighter pilots, Jewish war veterans, constables, culinary workers, firefighters and policemen. As a matter of fact, it would be much simpler to compose a roster of those organizations and businesses that *have not* at one time of another answered Opportunity Village's call for help.

Hillary Rodham Clinton, in her 1996 book, *It Takes a Village . . .*, may have said it best: "Each of us participates in several of the interlocking layers of the village. Each of us, therefore, has . . . opportunities and responsibilities . . ." These words apply not only to the children of the village, who Clinton was writing about, but also to all of its vulnerable, less fortunate members.

The Las Vegas community has recognized its responsibility to Opportunity Village and its citizens, and the community has never failed to answer the call.

Big supporters of Opportunity Village for many years, the Las Vegas Food & Beverage Workers Union (on the right) serve up a sumptuous Thanksgiving feast for clients and staff.

The National Association of Women in Construction, Las Vegas chapter, present a check to CCARC president Dessie Bailey in this 1963 newspaper article. The group is one of hundreds that have provided support over the years.

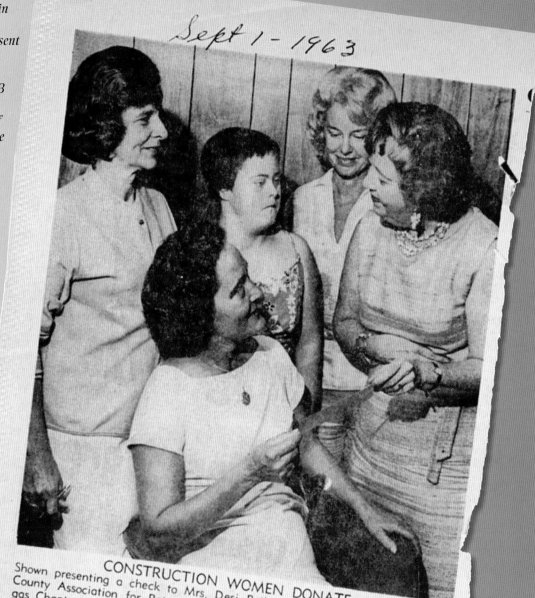

Sept 1 - 1963

CONSTRUCTION WOMEN DONATE

Shown presenting a check to Mrs. Desi Bailey seated, president, Clark County Association for Retarded Children is president elect of the Las Vegas Chapter, National Association of Women in Construction from left, Margaret Hart; Claudia Bailey; Joyce Beckett, president; and Mary Flowers, treasurer. Women In Construction is comprised of women directly employed in the construction industry and its relative trades. It is a non-profit organization and has as its goals a better understanding of the industry., service to the community, and a better understanding of what goes into the growth of a community from a construction standpoint. The Chapter will support the Clark County Association for Retarded Children during the ensuing year.

Review-Journal Photo

August 22, 1953

Jack Cortez'
Fabulous
LAS VEGAS
Magazine

"THE HEART OF SHOW BUSINESS"

ATTEND THE 4th ANNUAL "NIGHT OF STARS"

MONDAY AUGUST 24

CASHMAN FIELD... 8 P.M.
TICKETS
1.00 • 2.00
5.00 • 25.00
SPONSORED BY
VARIETY CLUB
TENT 39

CHIEF BARKER
JAKE KOZLOFF

PROCEEDS GO TO
SCHOOL FOR
HANDICAPPED
CHILDREN

No. 379

VARIETY CLUB OF
SOUTHERN NEVADA
INSTALLATION DINNER

ANNUAL INSTALLATION DINNER
TENT No. 39
Variety Club of Southern Nevada
PROUDLY PRESENTS
JACK BENNY WITH **JANE POWELL**
FLAMINGO HOTEL, TUESDAY, DECEMBER 4, 1951

DINNER AT 7:30
Tariff, $12.50 per Person

INFORMAL
PROCEEDS TO "HEART FUND"

Above: *An early Night of Stars program cover.*
Right: *A ticket to the Variety Club's first Night of Stars entertainment event. Both, courtesy Variety, The Children's Charity.*

CHAPTER ELEVEN

The Big Event:
Santas to Sequins

SOUND: Use bright Hollywood fanfare.

Guess who will be master of ceremonies at the gala benefit revue,
Tuesday night in the Flamingo Room? It's none other than
the fabulous Jack Benny, live at the Hotel Flamingo!
The sparkling array of stars is the who's who of show business . . .
Jack Benny . . . Jane Powell . . . Rafael Mendez, the greatest trumpet showman
. . . Gene Nelson, dancing star of "Painting the Clouds with Sunshine" . . .
plus the N.T.G. Calendar Girls with unique dance routines . . . and Michael
Edwards, singing the wonderful production numbers.
Next Tuesday night, the Flamingo Room will be stocked with stars . . . with
beauty . . . with superlative entertainment . . . and all proceeds to the "Heart"
fund . . . Variety's school for Handicapped Children. Tickets are $12.50 per person,
including dinner. Buy yours today at Flamingo's cashier cage or at the downtown
Golden Nugget.
— 30-second radio spot, KENO AM/FM, 1951

One of the hallmarks of Opportunity Village and its predecessor organization, CCARC, since its inception more than fifty years ago has been its prodigious fundraising ability. It is, quite simply, unequaled by any other not for profit organization in Nevada, and very possibly, not by any similar not for profit organization in the entire country.

They learned the techniques from the masters. Variety Clubs, self-dubbed "The Children's Charity," has been raising funds to support their child based charities since the 1920s. Tent 39, the Las Vegas Variety Club chapter, was granted its charter in 1950, with the express goal of establishing a school where disabled children would be welcome. Their first Big Event was held on July 31, 1950, and more than $10,000 was raised for the Heart Fund, the group's charitable arm. With the money, ground was broken for the Variety School for Handicapped Children. Although most of the labor for the construction of the school was donated by the various trade unions in town, a great deal of money was still required.

By year two, under the leadership of the group's first Head Barker (president) Ben Goffstein, assistant to the president of the Desert Inn, Tent 39 had mastered the techniques of fundraising in Las Vegas. There were actually two "annual" Variety Club fundraising events held in 1951, as the money was needed to fund the ongoing construction of the new school. The first one was held on June 11, 1951, at Cashman Field. Betty Hutton, Desi Arnez, Frankie Fontaine, and Les Paul & Mary Ford starred; and it was another grand success.

The second event in 1951 was scheduled for December fourth. Because of the winter date, it was set for the indoor Flamingo showroom at the fabulous Flamingo Hotel, and was combined with the club's annual installation banquet. Flamingo president Gus Greenbaum donated the dinners and the showroom. Las Vegas was home to many noted mobsters during this era, but Greenbaum, a member of the Chicago Outfit, and his associates were generous supporters of local charitable causes.

Jack Benny emceed the December revue, and he highlighted a star studded cast that included songstress and movie star Jane Powell, dancer Gene Nelson, and trumpet virtuoso Rafael Mendez, among many other acts. "Miss Powell captivated the hearts of the audience of some 600 with her beautiful voice and her charming stage manner," reported the **Las Vegas Review-Journal** the next morning. "She was very generous with her talents and sang half a dozen or more songs before leaving the stage."

In the ensuing years, the Night of Stars became the one must-see event each year. Almost every hotel in town lent their star performers for the evening, including such luminaries as the Dorsey Brothers, Mary Kaye Trio, Dick Haymes, Peggy Lee, Dorothy Collins, Ted Lewis, and Dan Dailey. Also appearing over the years were the Ritz Brothers, Joe E. Lewis, the Ames Brothers, Roberta Sherwood, Ken Murray, Marie Wilson, Tony Martin, Donald O'Connor, Lena Horne, Maurice Chevalier, and Sophie Tucker. Each event was an unrivaled lineup of stars.

An example of the broad participation by the Strip hotels is provided by this look at the 1953 lineup of stars:

The Dorsey Brothers, from the Last Frontier
Dick Haymes, from the Sands
Peggy Lee, from the Sahara
Dorothy Collins, from the Thunderbird
Mary Kaye Trio, from the Last Frontier
Joe E. Lewis, from the El Rancho
Ted Lewis and his orchestra, from the Desert Inn
John Charles Thomas and his singers, from the Flamingo.

This star-studded 1953 cast netted $15,000 for the Variety Club's school.

Summing up the 1953 show, the **Las Vegas Sun** wrote words that could have applied to any year: "The nation's top entertainment figures sparkled at Cashman Field last night before . . . the largest crowd ever together in Las Vegas, some 8,000 persons." "A

Left: *Famed band leaders Tommy and Jimmy Dorsey performed at the Variety Club's 1953 Night of Stars.* Below: *Film star Dan Dailey and singer Peggy Lee entertained at the 1953 Night of Stars. Both courtesy Variety, The Children's Charity.*

wonderful show for a wonderful cause." the *Las Vegas Review-Journal* added.

Variety Club's Night of Stars would go on to thrill locals — and a growing number of visitors, who came to town just to attend the spectacular — for many more years, finally ending its run in the late 1970s or early 1980s. Today, renamed Variety, The Children's Charity, the organization still supports the Las Vegas school that carries its name. They donate needed equipment to the school, and fill in other gaps within the community to support children's causes.

Most of Opportunity Village's Big Events are originals, but like any successful fundraising group, they don't shy away from a great idea if somebody else has it first. Such is the case with the most recent Big Event to become part of Opportunity Village's sparkling lineup.

"The Great Santa Run" was first held in 2001 in Newtown, Wales, in Great Britain. Co-sponsored by the city and District-Dial-A-Ride, a transport service for the disabled and elderly, the event immediately caught on. "Me and me mate took part," said one

participant, "Santa Run was a bloody great success." Another runner added, "Where else in the world will you ever see over 4,000 men, women, children and dogs dress up as Santa and run for four and a half miles, all for charity."

Four thousand Santas, indeed! As a matter of fact, Newtown's 2004 run featured 4,260 Santas taking up the challenge, enough to land the event in the Guinness Book of Records for the "World's Largest Santa Gathering."

None of this, of course, was missed by Opportunity Village's razor sharp fundraising department, where a chance to make some serious money and perhaps set a world's record at the same time was simply too good to pass up. And so the planning began.

Las Vegas has been home to the Las Vegas Marathon for a number of years, but the event has never achieved the status of the Boston Marathon,

Two thousand six hundred Santas turned for the First Annual Santa Run in 2005. In 2006, almost 4,000 Santas participated.

the New York City Marathon, or any of the nation's other leading races. But in 2005, Las Vegas race organizers decided it was time to make a grab for the big time. The surest way to accomplish that feat, they decided, was to eschew the normal race route that steered the event through the outskirts of town, and run it smack-dab through the middle of one of the world's most famous cities. And so the marathon course was designed; it would become the first race to run the entire world famous Las Vegas Strip, from one end to the other, through Glitter Gulch, the famed downtown Las Vegas hotel/casino corridor, and both begin and end on the Strip. Mandalay Bay . . . Luxor . . . MGM Grand . . . New York New York . . . Paris Las Vegas . . . Bellagio . . . Caesars Palace . . . Flamingo Hilton . . . Treasure Island . . . Venetian . . . Wynn Resorts . . . Stardust . . . Circus Circus . . . Sahara . . . Stratosphere . . . all of the largest, most luxurious

hotels in the world would become a backdrop for Las Vegas Marathon runners, while a spectacular laser display set to Elvis' "Viva Las Vegas" rocked in the background!

The race was scheduled for December 4, 2005; and it became immediately obvious to Opportunity Village planners that they had to tie into the marathon with their first Great Santa Run. Race officials cooperated, and although the two events were not officially joined, the Great Santa Run was allowed to take place the day before the marathon, on December third.

With visions of a Guinness Record dancing in their heads, a whole bunch of Santas braved a chilly morning and began lining up early. The first 4,500 Santas to register would receive a five piece Santa costume, complete with a tall red hat and white beard, as part of their $35 to $75 registration fee. The 4.5 mile course (this was no wimpy 3K run, mind you) provided a light spirited warm up for marathon runners, and a chance to become part of something R-E-A-L-L-Y important for less serious participants.

Sadly, the first Las Vegas Great Santa Run fell short. Only 2,600 Santas showed up to run, walk or saunter over the course, and Guinness officials left town with no new record to publish. A failure? You decide: $100,000 was raised, and 2,600 new friends of Opportunity Village had the time of their lives.

Undaunted, Opportunity Village staff and volunteers are already working on the next race. After all, they still have 1,900 Santa costumes in storage.

Reviewing the hundreds and hundreds of events Opportunity Village has staged over its fifty-three year history, none have had the impact, either financially or emotionally, of the "Concert of Love."

This gala affair, staged an unparalleled twenty-nine times from 1976 to 2002, became as much a part of the fabric of Las Vegas as Elvis Presley, glittering neon, and sumptuous buffets. It was, in short, quintessential Las Vegas.

Every event, every fundraiser, is a team effort. It takes dozens of dedicated, hardworking men and women to make each one successful. So it would normally be unjust to single out one person for most of the credit for any event. But the case of the Concerts of Love is unique, in that one man will always be remembered as the heart and soul of this long-running, fundraising Big Event. That man is Glenn Smith, and in Las Vegas, his name is synonymous with the Concert of Love.

Glenn Smith was born in Toronto, Canada, in 1950. As a precocious five year old, he found his true calling, starring in his own Canadian television show, "Microphone Muffets." As he grew into his voice, Smith began touring Canada where he achieved a level of stardom rarely seen in so young a performer,

being named the Canadian Entertainer of the Year in 1970. Gigs in the United States followed, and the singer/composer/musician soon landed contracts in New York and Las Vegas. He celebrated his eighteenth birthday by opening at the Fremont Hotel in Las Vegas with co-star Wayne Newton, also eighteen at the time. The two became lifelong friends.

In 1968 in Toronto, the strikingly handsome singer met a beautiful blonde dancer and TV commercial actress who was starring in her own weekly Canadian television show, "It's Happening." Linda Christopher immediately won Glenn's heart, and less than a year later the couple married. Linda Smith eventually gave up her dancing and acting career to become a wife.

In 1971, while Glenn Smith was on tour in the States, and nearly a month earlier than their doctor's estimate, Linda gave birth to their first child, a son they named Christopher.

Christopher was a Down syndrome baby.

The young couple was devastated, and they were torn by conflicting opinions on what they should do with their new baby. Finally, they decided upon the same path Roy Rogers and Dale Evans had chosen twenty year earlier: they would keep their baby, and they would love him unconditionally.

"Christopher has made us more compassionate and charitable people," Glenn Smith told the *Las Vegas Sun* in 1984. Proof of that statement first came when their son was only a year old. They had discovered there was no day care program available in Toronto for small children with disabilities, and they were determined to start one. To raise money, the young couple decided to stage a concert in 1972. They first planned to borrow a church basement in which to stage the event, but they hadn't counted on the loving help they received from some show business friends.

Two good friends, Wayne Newton and Glenn Smith, prepare for the 1979 Concert of Love, at the Frontier Hotel.

The musical *Godspell* was appearing in town, and three good friends, Gilda Radner, Martin Short and Paul Schaeffer were starring. They volunteered to help out, and a 3,000 seat auditorium was arranged for the show, which they decided to call "Concert of Love, " in son Chris's honor. Linda Smith sold tickets and promoted the show, promising everybody their money back if they weren't completely satisfied. The concert was a sellout; Glenn's performance was magical, and Radner, Short, and Schaeffer had a grand time doing the show. Most importantly, an idea was born.

The next four Concerts of Love were staged by the Smiths in Canada and upstate New York, with the proceeds each year going to the national organization Association of Retarded Children, or ARC.

By 1976, Glenn Smith was spending nearly half of his time performing in Las Vegas showrooms and lounges. The couple decided they needed to settle down, and put Chris in a good school where he could thrive. So Glenn, Linda, and Chris moved permanently to Las Vegas, bringing their successful Concert of Love with them. Chris went on to attend the Variety School, then the Helen J. Stewart School; and has been a well-adjusted, happy client at Opportunity Village ever since.

From 1977 through 2003, the Concert of Love became part of Las

A Mike Smith cartoon depicts Glenn Smith and his small son Chris.

Vegas entertainment history, with all proceeds each year dedicated to Opportunity Village. A staggering four million dollars was raised by the concerts over the years.

The format of the fabulously successful show was established early, and rarely altered. Linda Smith was the producer; Glenn Smith was always the lead act. A multi-talented performer, he sings and plays four instruments, in addition to being a composer and lyricist. Entertainment writers who have attended a Concert of Love, which are usually standing-room-only shows, also remark about Glenn Smith's magnetic stage persona.

Each show also featured one big-name star, and a rousing production number. The lineup of stars over the years is the stuff of legend: Wayne Newton (eight times,) Tom Jones, Englebert Humperdink, Ann-Margaret, Gladys Knight, Dionne Warwick, Bill Cosby, Chicago, Cirque du Soleil, the Righteous Brothers, Rich Little, and Tony Orlando to mention but a few.

Glenn Smith's
CONCERT of Love

FROM THE HEART.

NINETEENTH ANNUAL
GLENN SMITH
CONCERT OF LOVE
TO BENEFIT
OPPORTUNITY VILLAGE
TROPICANA
RESORT AND CASINO
TIFFANY THEATER
AT 1:30 P.M.

NINETEENTH ANNUAL
GLENN SMITH
CONCERT OF LOVE
TO BENEFIT
OPPORTUNITY VILLAGE
♥
TROPICANA
RESORT AND CASINO
TIFFANY THEATER
SUNDAY, MARCH 13TH AT 1:30 P.M.
DOORS OPEN AT 12:00 P.M.
BENEFACTOR ♥ ADMIT ONE
DONATIONS OVER $15 ARE MADE TO OPPORTUNITY VILLAGE,
A RECOGNIZED 501(c)(3) CHARITY.

The Tropicana Resort and Casino
presents

Glenn Smith
in the 19th Annual Concert of Love
for the benefit of
OPPORTUNITY VILLAGE

Starring
The Righteous Brothers

♥

Rich Little

♥

Featuring
Les Folies Bergere

♥

Cirque du Soleil's Mystère

♥

Announcer
Steve Schorr

Production and Direction
provided by Dick Foster Productions

Producer Lynn Foster
Director David Gravatt

Associate Producer Mike Cody
Special Events Marie Cody

Executive Producer Linda Smith

BIG DREAMS

BIGGER HEARTS

24TH ANNUAL GLENN SMITH
CONCERT of LOVE
FOR THE BENEFIT
OF OPPORTUNITY VILLAGE

Left: *A program cover for the twenty-fourth annual Glenn Smith Concert of Love, held in 1999.*

By the late 1990s, Glenn and Linda had divorced, but continued to jointly put on the Concert of Love. But the Las Vegas entertainment scene was changing. It had become a corporate town, showroom policies were very different from the early days, and Las Vegas entertainment itself was undergoing a fundamental shift away from star performers. The 2003 Concert of Love at the Rio Hotel became the Smiths' last "annual" affair.

Gone for good? Unlikely. "We hope to continue them," Linda Smith said recently. They are currently considering putting on their next concert in 2008 when Opportunity Village celebrates its fifty-fifth anniversary. So when all the stars once again become perfectly aligned in the heavens, Las Vegas locals and visitors might have another chance to attend a Concert of Love. If so, you can make a safe bet it will be another sold-out, knock-out show!

♥ ♥ ♥

Over the years, many of Opportunity Village's most successful fundraising events have come to them as gifts from within the Las Vegas community, a surprisingly caring and giving citizenry. The Great Meatball Festival was such an event.

The Boulevard Mall was Las Vegas' first fully enclosed regional mall. Through its earlier history, one of its tenants was the Vineyard Restaurant, an Italian eatery that was for years a favorite locals' dining spot. In the late 1970s a young man from Syracuse, New York, moved to town to manage the restaurant for its New York owners, Charlie Zades, Guido Iacovelli and Tony Mincolla. Jack Sheridan was a community minded man, and immediately began volunteering at Opportunity Village. Over time he decided to stage an annual event to raise funds for the

Glenn Smith, who had a fabulously successful twenty-eight year run with his Concert of Love, in support of Opportunity Village, hugs his son Chris at the 2002 event.

organization, and his brainchild, the Great Meatball Festival, was born.

As Sheridan told the *Las Vegas Sun* in 1985, "Our idea was to provide an atmosphere of fun, some food and contests, to raise money for Opportunity Village." It succeeded on all three counts beyond anyone's expectations. From its first run in 1982, through its ninth and last annual appearance in 1990, the Great Meatball Festival became one of Opportunity Village's most successful fundraisers.

It was an all-day affair, held in the mall parking lot, with a carnival atmosphere. Local businesses and service groups rented booths, with thirty-five to forty included each year, and food and games were the

A bevy of brightly attired ladies handed out beads to guests at the last Concert of Love.

The 1st Annual
Great Meatball Festival,
Fancy Bike Contest
& Parade

Sponsored By
The Vineyard Restaurant
to benefit Opportunity Village

LOOK INSIDE
FOR YOUR GUIDE
TO GOOD TIMES!!

Visit our
booths for fun
games & fun

COME ONE · COME

The meat of the matter

Toru Kawana/Review-Journal

Lance Alexander of radio station KOMP wolfs down meatballs during the "Media Meatball Eating" contest at the Boulevard Mall Sun- day. TV station KBLR, Channel 39, won the event, which aided Opportunity Village, a skills training center for the handicapped.

A media contestant stuffs another meatball into his mouth during the meatball easting contest at the Great Meatball Festival. Left: *The Great Meatball Festival cartoon mascot.*

main order of business. Games included a pie-in-the-face booth, wheel of fortune, beanbag toss, milk bottle toss, pony rides, and a dunk tank. But the most popular booth became the cow chip throwing contest. "Prime cow chips have been imported from Moapa Valley and other parts unknown," The **Las Vegas Review-Journal** boasted with tongue in cheek in 1985; "They have been carefully chosen for texture, hue, originality . . . and balance."

A walk-a-thon became part of the day, with participants selling sponsorship to friends and co-workers for $10 a pop. The first year, a parade was also included, but it was soon dropped for being too time consuming. But the highlight of each year's event was undoubtedly the media meatball eating contest. Up to three dozen three-man teams from radio, television,

magazines and newspapers competed against each other — and against the clock — to devour a pan of thirty meatballs. The tasty chore could generally be completed in less than sixty seconds, but not without a great deal of the spicy Italian treats ending up on the faces of the competitors.

Sheridan was once asked why he contributed so much of his personal time, energy, and money to Opportunity Village. His simple answer was to the point, "What goes around, comes around." Upon reflection, he added, "I've been at the employment training center, and I know where the money they raise goes. It's really the only community charity we have in Las Vegas." Sheridan said he also hired Opportunity Village clients for the restaurant, and used the Opportunity Village print shop to emblazon the Vineyard Restaurant logo on tee shirts.

Over the nine year run of the Great Meatball Festival, more than $100,000 found its way into Opportunity Village's treasury, and thousand of local families enjoyed a bit of small town ambience for at least one day a year . . . to say nothing of the annual bout of indigestion suffered by most local media types.

♥ ♥ ♥

Another long standing fundraiser is "Miss Kitty's Jeans to Jewels," an old fashion western hoedown and BBQ that, in 2006, celebrated its fourteenth annual run.

The "Miss Kitty" after whom the event is named is Kitty Rodman, one of Opportunity Village's most ardent supporters for more than a half century. Rodman is also one of the city's most generous philanthropists. A partner in Sierra Construction Corp., Rodman's firm built projects for the Atomic Energy Commission, Nellis Air Force Base, Clark County School District, University of Nevada Las Vegas, and numerous hotel resorts.

Jeans to Jewels annually attracts between 600 to 800 of the city's leading social, political, business and philanthropic citizens. For the first five years, the event was held at the home of Opportunity Village Advisory Board member John Wasserburger, the five acre J. W. Ranch. However, when the event grew too large for that venue, it was moved to the Bitter Root Ranch in northeast Las Vegas, a working cutting horse ranch belonging to Frank and Bonnie Martin, also longtime supporters of the organization.

Nevada's U.S. Senator John Ensign is honorary chairman of the event each year.

Dressed to the "nines" in cowboy finery, guests enjoy entertainment, dancing, and great western grub, as well as an exciting cutting horse demonstration. There are also games for the younger cowboy and cowgirl set. One of the highlights of the event is a silent auction, featuring very generous items donated by area businesses and Opportunity Village supporters.

The event has raised close to

Above: *An invitation to Miss Kitty's Jeans to Jewels, one of Opportunity Village's longest running fund raising events. A colorful sign announces Miss Kitty's Jeans to Jewels BBQ and hoedown event at the Bitter Root Ranch.*

Top: *Bonnie (from left) and Frank Martin, and Miss Kitty Rodman, welcome guests to the annual Miss Kitty's Jeans to Jewels fundraiser at the Martin's ranch.* Middle: *Children's sack races are a lot of fun at the annual Jeans to Jewels fundraiser.* Bottom: *Hundreds of Las Vegas's most prominent citizens gather annually to raise funds for the organization at Miss Kitty's Jeans to Jewels fundraiser.*

$2,000,000 for Opportunity Village coffers since its inception.

♥ ♥ ♥

A number of other big events played a prominent part in Opportunity Village's long fundraising history, but have now become a part of the past. The Turkey Trot was one such event.

If there exists a continuum of racing events, from the most serious to the most frivolous, the Las Vegas Marathon certainly stands near the earnest end of the line, while the Great Santa Race would be perched comfortably at the opposite end. Somewhere between the two on the continuum would be the Turkey Trot.

Dorothy Huffey

ON THE SCENE

From jewels to jeans ... It was mighty fine evening honoring Kitty Rodman for the May 22 benefit for Opportunity Village. The western round-up took place at the Paradise Valley spread of John Wasserburger. The sellout crowd enjoyed bidding on 67 unique items such as a boot filled with silver dollars, your name in neon lights, Leiber and Escada purses, Roy Purcell and LeRoy Neiman art, IGT Poker machine, and beautiful jewelry. Lippizaner horses performed in the ring and line dancing to the music of Silverado had everyone foot stompin' till the cows came home. Palace Station provided the chuckwagon dinner, and desserts were by Milan Bakery. Many thanks to Sherry Adler and her fine committee of Shari Compton-Smith, Gloria Fine, Judy Kostelecky, Michele Rebar, Linda Richardson, Jane Schorr, Linda Smith, Kaye Walden and Mel Turner of IATSE Local 720 for getting everything donated. Proceeds will benefit Opportunity Village's full-time vocational and educational programs for the mentally retarded.

Inaugurated in the early 1980s, the race was co-sponsored by KTNV channel 13, the local ABC affiliate, and the *Las Vegas Review-Journal*. In about year five, the local telephone company also joined as a co-sponsor. Originally, it was planned that each year a new benefactor organization would receive the proceeds from the event, but the chemistry between Opportunity Village and the two sponsors was good, so it remained the sole benefactor for the next dozen or so years.

The race took place each year during Thanksgiving week, thus the name Turkey Trot. The 10k (6.2 mile) race, augmented by a two mile fun run, was very high on the Las Vegas family entertainment radar for its entire history. As a 1986 story in the *Las Vegas Review-Journal* reported, "It was encouraging to see so many dads out there running with their sons and moms with their daughters. Lots of babies were also getting free rides over both the two mile and 10k courses."

In its earliest years, the Turkey Trot drew 1,000 to 1,500 runners, but toward the end of its history, 2,500 to 3,000 runners participated. While the new Las Vegas Marathon now runs the entire length of the famed Las Vegas Strip, it was not the first race to compete on the resort lined, neon studded corridor. That honor belongs to the Turkey Trot, which each year included the northern portion of the Strip on its course.

The event had never been Opportunity Village's largest fundraiser, donating between $15,000 and $20,000 each year. But it was a source of steady income, and Opportunity Village received great press exposure thanks to the media sponsors. But the Turkey Trot eventually gave way to progress in the late 1990s. Opportunity Village was now devoting most of its time and efforts to the Magical Forest, which had become the organization's largest fundraiser; and sponsors decided to pull the plug on the event. But it was sure fun while it lasted.

A newspaper ad for the annual Turkey Trot Run in 1991.

♥ ♥ ♥

Some ideas explode full blown all at once, like a beautiful flower that suddenly opens and exposes all its beauty, color, and grandeur in an instant. Other ideas begin like the humble acorn, and take time to develop into the thing of beauty and majesty that becomes a giant oak. Such was the case with the Magical Forest, the big event to end all big events, that began ever so slowly but has developed into one of the most fabulous fundraising events in Las Vegas history.

It all began quite simply, in December 1991. The first large building on the West Oakey campus had just been completed, occupying two of the plot's six acres at the far eastern end of the property. Linda Smith, the group's chief development officer, decided to have a reception in the new gymnasium to thank all the donors and in-kind contributors who had paid for the building. Because Christmas was approaching, Smith decided to decorate and light all the beautiful pine trees on the property to make it more festive. On the rather barren western end of the property, they brought in potted trees to carry out the look. Kids from Bonanza High School donated their time to light and decorate all the trees, and when it was finished, everyone, including Smith, was amazed at how beautiful it looked.

"That evening, when our guests began pulling into the lot, they were charmed," Smith said. "Later, as people were leaving the reception, they stopped and asked if we could leave the lights on so they could bring their children back to see them." Smith agreed.

For the next few weeks, everybody was stunned at the number of cars that arrived nightly to see the lights. "This wasn't a fundraiser," Smith admitted; "it was a friend raiser." People were asking, "What is this Opportunity Village? Who are they?" and lots of people were discovering the group and its work for the first time.

Never one to miss a chance to make some money, Smith found an old wishing well, one of many the group had used years earlier to solicit donations throughout the city, and she put it out amid the lighted trees. She also began making hot chocolate in the new kitchen, and had her mother bake cookies, which they sold from a small food stand.

By the time the holiday season was over, and they had counted the proceeds, everybody was amazed to learn that over 2,000 people had visited, and $3,000 had been raised. More importantly, an idea had been born.

For the following year, board member and local developer Brett Torino volunteered labor from his crew and his subcontractors, and they built some permanent structures to house various Christmas displays. That second year, $60,000 was raised, and by the third year, the figure had swelled to $120,000. The Magical Forest was off and running, and it has never looked back.

In 2005, Magical Forest was visited by more than 150,000 people, and grossed $1,450,000. A study conducted during the event showed that one out of four visitors came from out of state.

Today, Magical Forest is a virtual Christmas theme park. Two 32-passenger trains, dubbed the Forest Express, circle the entire four-and-a-half acre event

The walkway to the Magical Forest is awash with bright holiday lights. The Magical Forest is a magical place for local residents. Area businesses host displays at the annual Magical Forest, like this one from Dick Foster Productions at right, and Krispy Kreme, opposite page.

DICK FOSTER PRODUCTIONS

North Pole

What's Christmas without Santa Claus?

site, offering an open air view of everything that's going on. The beautiful carousel, with its whimsical horses gaily moving up and down to the sounds of laughing children, attracts throngs of people. A large log cabin houses gift booths, the works of local artisans and craftsmen, and two castles loom high overhead. More than fifty other booths and attractions await excited visitors, all sitting amid the wooded forest, with more 3,000,000 lights sparkling above.

The Walk of the Arches is comprised of twenty-five huge archways festooned with garlands and lights providing a magical canopy for strolling families. In 2006 the Walk was expanded to fifty archways. A gingerbread exhibit, held in the Gingerbread Ballroom, displays dozens of tasty works of art designed and built by some of the world's most talented chefs from large Strip resorts. Three choirs sing Christmas carols each night on the performance stage. A large whimsical firehouse invites children to enter the magical world of fireman, and next year an adjoining exhibit will be hosted by local police

agencies. And of course, watching over the entire forest from their own workshop, are Santa Claus and his elves waiting to greet the children.

The Magical Forest never stops growing. New for 2006 was a permanent food court, an Alpine slide where children can slide down artificial snow, and a "glice" figure skating and storytelling exhibit, a technology that creates a skating rink from glass and ice.

An event of this magnitude does not come together overnight. Planning begins the day the previous event closes down for the season, and continues all year. Heading up the event is the organization's sole employee dedicated just to the Magical Forest; he's dubbed "the king of the forest." His name is Jack Sheridan, and yes, he's the same Jack Sheridan who created the very successful Great Meatball Festival nearly a quarter century earlier. When the Vineyard Restaurant closed its doors for good, Sheridan opened his own business, The Butler Did It catering service. But when an opening occurred to run the Magical Forest, he couldn't pass it up, and he joined the Opportunity Village staff.

Sheridan and the other Opportunity Village staffers aren't alone in their work, however. Once again, the business community coalesces in a big way to volunteer their services to make each year's event bigger and better than the year before. Many of the largest and most influential construction and development companies join in: Marnell Carran Associates, designers and builders of many of the famous Las Vegas Strip's largest resort/hotels; the prestigious JMA Architects; Pulte Homes, one of the nation's largest home builders; Bombard Electric, the huge electrical contracting firm; and Martin Harris Construction

Company, another builder of some of the city's leading resorts. They are joined by dozens of other firms, large and small, in the planning and execution of the project.

"It's amazing." Linda Smith said. "At these planning meetings, you'd think we were building the Mirage Hotel. It's that level of involvement . . . they roll out these architectural plans and it'll be, instead of the Wynn Resorts, this gingerbread-looking castle."

Over the entire year, Smith estimates, as many as a thousand volunteers may be involved in pulling the event together and manning it during its five week run.

It is indeed a "Magical" Forest.

♥ ♥ ♥

Another significant event also occurs annually, and serves as the kickoff for the Magical Forest. It's called appropriately, Camelot.

Camelot is a formal gala held to thank the organization's most significant benefactors. Limited to 450 people, the event is one of the city's premier VIP social events. The very top elite of the city's business, professional, political and social world attend, and get the year's first look at Magical Forest.

Smith admits there was initially some apprehension over whether the event would work. "We worried if these people would dress up in black tie and attend a party held in a gym," she said. But attend they did. The event sells out every year, usually many months in advance. "People of influence love that they can

Bagpipers entertain at the annual Camelot fundraising gala.

come to a formal party and not have to pass by slot machines," she said. There was even some consideration of moving to one of the hotels to grow the capacity, but wiser heads recognized that the exclusivity of the limited size of the event added to its luster.

Those who are fortunate enough to be able to purchase tickets at $500 a person, or $5,000 per table, enjoy cocktails and a fabulous dinner prepared by famed Strip hotel chefs, before attending opening night in the Magical Forest. Cocktail waitresses, bartenders, waiters, busboys, kitchen help, and all the other necessary support staff give up their lucrative Saturday night shifts to donate their time to make the gala event a big success.

A daring fire-eater was another 'hot' performer at the Camelot fundraising gala.

Below: *World famous chefs from the city's leading hotel/resorts join together to prepare a lavish dinner for celebrants at the annual Camelot dinner dance, which formally opens the Magical Forest each year.*

Las Vegas entertainers Siegfried & Roy co-sponsored a Celebrity Bear Auction.

Everybody agrees the medieval themed event is a smash hit year after year. And, not coincidentally, the event raises more than a $250,000 annually for Opportunity Village.

♥ ♥ ♥

During the 1970s and 1980s, a number of charity horseshows were held, sponsored by longtime area car dealer Fletcher Jones Sr. Many of the finest horses from all over the Southwest competed in the events, held about a half-dozen times over the two decades.

In 2002, Opportunity Village partnered with noted Strip magicians and entertainers, Siegfried & Roy, to hold a Celebrity Bear Auction. Sponsored by high-end department store, Nieman Marcus, the auction featured teddy bears personally autographed by a long list of A-level celebrities: Tom Cruise, Brad Pitt, Cher, Anthony Hopkins, and Whoopie Goldberg, to mention just a few. The event was planned as an annual affair, but soon after it launched Roy Horn suffered a terrible accident, from which he is steadily recovering. So don't count out this event for the future.

Jazz concerts . . . fashion shows . . . celebrity chef cooking shows . . . haunted houses . . . superstar concerts . . . star studded galas . . . there is truly no end to the kind of events that have been held over the years to advance Opportunity Village's agenda. And, as we look to the future, in the words of one old wag, "You ain't seen nothin' yet!"

Opportunity Village presents

"An American Musical High" Fashion Show and Luncheon

SATURDAY, MARCH 13
12 NOON
HACIENDA HOTEL SHOWROOM
tickets $10

**Co-Produced by
Monnet Alvarez and Colleen
Shroeder of the Broadway**

Ticket Information 384-8170

The Show will feature
Spectacular Fashions at
Bargain Prices
(from $5.00 to $40.00)

Fashions will be on sale to the public immediately following the show in the Granada Room of the Hacienda at 2:30

Carolyn Everette
One of the fashion models to be seen in "American Musical High Fashion Show"

An ad for one of the Vanguard Club's rollicking second-hand clothing fashion shows in the early 1980s.
Right: The first business license issued to the Clark County Association for Retarded Children, the forerunner of Opportunity Village, for their North Las Vegas Thrift Shop.

CHAPTER TWELVE

The Economics:
A Dollar Here,
A Dollar There

Forty-five years ago, in 1962, Clark County Association for Retarded Children (CCARC), the forerunner of Opportunity Village, went into business for the first time.

The eight year old organization, then under the presidency of founder Dessie Bailey, acquired a business license from the city of North Las Vegas to open and operate a thrift store. That was the group's first entry into the world of high finance, and set a standard that has become the envy of not-for-profit groups around the country ever since.

Prior to that time, from its initial founding in 1954, CCARC had relied for its funding on private donations and its own small neighborhood enterprises: garage sales, bake sales, car washes and similar grassroots events. But it had become obvious that new revenue streams were imperative if the group was to continue the funding of its children's education program. That initial foray into business was a bell-wether of things to come, but it was also a standalone success, raising more than $10,000 in its first year.

Only a few years after the launching of the North Las Vegas thrift shop, the group's first executive director, Dr. Ted Johnson, laid out his plans for a future that included a variety of business ventures to fund the many activities he envisioned would be needed to support Clark County's growing population of people with mental retardation. His dream took a number of years to develop, but a turning point occurred in 1981.

An article in the *Las Vegas Review-Journal* on September 16, 1981 carried a headline that surprised thousands of local readers: "Opportunity Village Leaves United Way." The timing for such a move was bewildering. President Reagan's budget tightening had already threatened a cutback in federal funding for the nation's not-for-profits, and now, according to the article, Opportunity Village was pulling out of an agency that had pledged $75,000 to its support. It appeared to be either a very brave or a very foolish move by the organization's leaders.

"The board of directors felt they had to go out on their own and expand the fundraising base," executive director Jerry Allen was quoted in the article as saying. "United Way was not able to provide us with the funding we needed to expand." Allen went on to explain that there was absolutely no rift between the two agencies, that the move was simply a matter of financial survival. Participation in United Way dictated how its member agencies could raise funds, and Opportunity Village felt the rules were too restrictive.

At the time, the group's revenue came from a combination of federal and state funding, donations and grants, a few annual fundraising events like Glenn Smith's Concert of Love, and their thrift stores sales. That was it. It was at this time, and as part of this plan, that Linda Smith was hired as the agency's first professional fund raiser, a story told in chapter six.

Thus the fundraising began. It received a huge boost just two years later when Opportunity Village secured its first federal work contract. It was from Nellis Air Force Base, that nearly twenty years later would again hire the organization to fulfill all its food service requirements. But that first contract was much more humble, a $337,000 commitment. Twenty-five clients were put to work stocking the base's commissary shelves.

The clients were daily driven to the base, where they were taught to move items from the warehouse to the commissary, stack them neatly on the correct shelves, price them, and keep the shelves neat and orderly. They were also charged with cleaning the commissary. "It's a high volume operation," executive director Jerry Allen said at the time. "We put up approximately 54,000 cases of merchandise on the shelves over the span of a month."

Allen reported that the biggest fear going into the contract was that the clients, who had never worked at night before, would have trouble adjusting to a night shift operation. As it turned out, the clients adjusted beautifully; it was the supervisory staff that had trouble adjusting.

That contract was a launching pad for "mainstreaming" people with intellectual disabilities into the Southern Nevada workforce. It was a huge success. The U.S. Air Force's Inspector General inspected the premises a few months after the inauguration of the contract, and pronounced it the cleanest commissary he'd ever seen. Nellis personnel credited the clients with helping them achieve record sales in the commissary.

It is a shame that Dessie Bailey and Ted Johnson are not here today to see what they gave birth to. From those humble beginnings, Opportunity Village has become an unparalleled not-for-profit success story.

♥ ♥ ♥

The purpose of this chapter is not to detail and explain the entire financial structure of Opportunity Village. That would make dry, cumbersome reading. Anyone interested in the minutiae of the financial information can go to the organization's web site at www.opportunityvillage.org where the most recent fiscal year statements are reproduced. The information is not confidential. It must be made public by law.

The person in charge of financial matters is Randy Sibbett, Director of Administrative Services. His responsibilities include not only overseeing the financial side of the organization but also security, facilities, and information technology. Sibbett has been with Opportunity Village for approximately six years.

Like so many other people in executive positions within the organization, Sibbett joined the company not only for the challenge of the work but also for the mission. "A niece and a nephew on my wife's side of the family were born with Down syndrome," he said. After moving to Las Vegas from Sacramento, Sibbett had two job offers simultaneously. "I had two equal opportunities, so the mission was what swung it," he said.

Looking at Opportunity Village's finances is confounded by the fact that the organization is composed of two separate corporations, one primarily involved in operations and the other in fundraising. Any figures discussed in the following text, whenever necessary and unless otherwise noted, are combined figures from both corporations.

For the most recent twelve month period available when this book was being prepared, the twelve months ending February 2006, Opportunity Village

From those humble beginnings, Opportunity Village has become an unparalleled not for profit success story.

had gross income from all sources of $22,407,977, and gross expenses of $17,552,973.

The fact that an organization is classified by the Internal Revenue Service as not-for-profit does not mean it cannot earn a profit. It simply means that whatever profit is earned is not paid out to owners or stockholders; it is retained internally to be spent for the advancement of the organization's mission. In the case of Opportunity Village, earning a profit is very important. It is that money that allows them to improve the services offered to their clients, and to serve an ever growing population of people with mental retardation.

Looking at a breakdown of the "income" side of the ledger from the most recent twelve month period, provides some interesting contrasts: (figures rounded off)

$4,244,000	Government Support Payments
$6,080,000	Contributions and Grants (including in-kind contributions)
$1,978,000	Fundraising Activities
$6,328,000	Service Contracts
$616,000	Document Destruction
$1,694,000	Employment Training Centers
$750,000	Retail Operations (the Thrift Store)
$718,000	All Other Income

The service contracts generated twenty-eight percent of all revenue. The fact that Opportunity Village provides employment, with a regular paycheck and attractive benefits, to hundreds of local men and women with disabilities speaks to the importance of that figure. When you add in the revenue generated by the employment training centers (eight percent), the document destruction business (three percent), and the retail operations (three percent), you find that forty-two percent of *all* the agency's income results from putting people with disabilities to work.

The fundraising efforts of Linda Smith's department are also reflected in the income figures: twenty-seven percent of total income from contributions and grants; and another nine percent from fundraising events.

The importance of the fundraising events to the organization's overall mission is only partially reflected in its numbers, however. Annual events like the Magical Forest— the group's largest fundraising event at over $1.5 millon — also puts a very public face on Opportunity Village. Thousands of local residents visit the event every Christmas season, and leave with a better understanding of the group's mission. There is absolutely no doubt that this positive public exposure helps channel money into the "contributions" category. Many visitors also become volunteers.

For most community based rehabilitation agencies like Opportunity Village, the income item labeled "government support" is where most of the agency's income is listed. Most survive thanks to their state government's support of its programs, which can amount from seventy-five to ninety percent of its income. That is not the case with Opportunity Village. As the foregoing figures indicate, government support represented only nineteen percent of the agency's total operating income, making it one of the most self-sufficient agencies of its type in the country.

This fact alone makes Opportunity Village unique. Because the organization is able to raise most of its own money, it is able to serve more people and provide a broader range of programs than other, similar organizations. More telling perhaps is the fact that the organization has saved taxpayers nearly one billion dollars over the past fifty years because of its self-sufficiency. It is this fact that is responsible for so many local businesses and businessmen lining up to support the organization. As one business leader said,

"I appreciate that Opportunity Village doesn't always have their hand out to the government for more funding. They raise their own money, and that's why I've always been willing to help out when I can."

This is certainly not to say that the government funds Opportunity Village receives are unimportant. They are very important. Most of these funds come from the State of Nevada, in the form of funding for those people with a disability who are undergoing vocational training. Most of the funds flow to the organization through the Desert Regional Center (DRC), an agency of the State Department of Human Resources' Division of Mental Health and Developmental Services.

Funds are allocated, through the legislature, based upon the client to staff ratio required for the training of each individual. For those clients at the very lowest functioning level, the term "vocational training" may be a misnomer. Some of these clients, like those in Project PRIDE, will never be able to work, thus the training is directed more toward teaching life skills, or at its basest level, simply assisting a client to get through the day.

At this most fundamental level, called Level 0, or "Supported Employment," the State pays $23.85 per hour, per client for one on one training. From this point on, all funding is figured on a per day, per client basis, Level 0 being the only one calculated on a per hour basis.

Level 2, or "Intensive Habilitation," is a client to staff ratio of 2:1, and pays $95.40 per day; Level 3, or "Habilitation," is 5:1 and pays $38.16 per day. Level 4, "Jobs Training/Training Center," is 8:1, and pays

$23.85 per day; and Level 9, "Habilitation," is 3:1 and pays $63.59 per day. There are other levels, but they do not enter into Opportunity Village's world. All of the foregoing rates were in effect as of July 1, 2005.

Each Opportunity Village client has been for the level of service he requires when he first enters the DRC system. Annual or periodic reviews can change that level of service if changes in the client's performance dictate.

For many years, Nevada ranked last among all the states in funding for services for people with disabilities. But, according to executive director Ed Guthrie, that all began to change about seven years ago when Governor Kenny Guinn and the Legislature passed into law Assembly Bill 513. That bill increased funding significantly for senior services, rural health services and services for people with disabilites. In order to simply reach the level of funding provided by most neighboring states, AB 513 had to increase funding by approximately thirty-eight percent, according to Guthrie.

"I don't believe we're last any longer," he said. "We may have made it all the way to forty-eighth out of fifty." Despite the jump, Guthrie emphasized that Nevada is still far behind most other states, a fact that has both positive and negative ramifications. On the negative side, the shortage of funding has obviously hurt organizations like Opportunity Village as they work toward their mission.

However, on the other side of the ledger, Guthrie said, "We've managed to make that problem, that challenge, into an opportunity. We've focused our

. . . government support represented only nineteen percent of the agency's total operating income, making it one of the most self-sufficient agencies of its type in the country.

efforts on seeing how self sufficient we can become without relying on state dollars."

Put in a different context, Guthrie said that if Opportunity Village had served the same number of clients in Utah, it would have received about $500,000 more in state funding last year. In California, that figure would have been closer to $1 million, he said.

Finally, it is an interesting exercise in growth to look at how some of the foregoing figures have changed over the past five years. (The figures for the year 2000 are fiscal year figures [July 1, 1999 — June 30, 2000] while the comparative figures are twelve months ending February 2006.)

| TOTAL INCOME | +249 percent |
| TOTAL EXPENSES | +246 percent |

Looking at a couple of breakdowns, we discover that service contract income has grown by +349 percent over the comparable period, an indication of the organization's growing reliance on its competition with the for-profit sector for job contracts.

Work center revenue has not grown nearly as fast. But this represents the organization's employment training centers, which are a mature product and not as liable to make dramatic gains as the more recent service contract business.

One other category, contributions and grants, also outperformed the averages, growing by +307 percent.

♥ ♥ ♥

It will be interesting to see how today's figures will compare with those from five years in the future. The third campus will be operating by then, and many more clients will be served. It's a safe bet, however, that no matter what happens, Opportunity Village will continue to be a model of self-sufficiency.

CHAPTER THIRTEEN

The Future:
We've Only Just Begun

In March 2006, eighty people in need of Opportunity Village's services moved into Clark County, Nevada. In April 2006, another eighty moved in, and in May 2006, another eighty.

Of course, these aren't actual numbers; they are averages. But what they mean is that in 2006 nearly 1,000 men, women and children with a disability that would qualify them for Opportunity Village's services moved into Clark County. In 2007, another 1,000 or so will move in, and as we look farther into the future, the number will increase.

Opportunity Village is well aware of these statistics. Throughout the entire organization, from the top man on down to the humblest employee, there is a realization that to serve its constituency, the organization must grow.

This, the final chapter in our look at this one-of-a-kind group, is a peek into the future.

♥ ♥ ♥

Of all the exciting developments going on at Opportunity Village, none can match the plans for the organization's new campus in the southwest portion of the valley at the corner of Buffalo Drive and Patrick Road. Here, on a prime 10.9 acre parcel will be the group's third major facility in Clark County.

Opportunity Village was able to lease the land in a rather unique two-way deal. The federal government's Bureau of Land Management, which owns seventy percent of all the land in Nevada, granted the parcel to Clark County's McCarran International Airport, and the County in turn agreed to lease it to Opportunity Village for thirty years, with a fifteen year renewal option, at an extremely attractive rate. This lucrative land deal was consummated in 2005 and design plans began immediately. The firm of JMA Architecture Studios has designed a beautiful campus with two state-of-the-art facilities that Opportunity Village hopes to have ready for service by late 2007.

The larger of the two buildings will be a 55,000 square foot employment training center that will serve 250 to 300 people every day. The smaller building will be a 28,000 square foot arts enrichment center, and will be open to all of the organization's clients from throughout Clark County.

The employment training center will be similar to the ones on the West Oakey and Henderson campuses, but with more space and more modern facilities. At the heart of the building will be vocational training facilities whose focus is on skill-building that will lead to more independent employment in the community at-large. Other clients will choose to remain at the employment training center for as long as necessary, some for a lifetime.

The employment training center will be supported by a spacious warehouse for onloading and offloading materials and supplies from the myriad of contracts the organization fulfills. This is a necessary component to insure efficiency in the operation, but a luxury the other two centers do not enjoy. There will also be vocational assessment rooms, offices, meeting space, and quiet rooms, all surrounding an open courtyard for dining, relaxing or meditation. A lunchroom will also be available to serve clients and staff.

State-of-the art facilities for Project PRIDE and Project ENABLE will also be part of the employment and training center, allowing those two vital programs to serve more residents than ever.

Interior décor will be bright and modern. Murals and wall coverings will feature colorful designs, providing visual stimulation in work spaces. A unique feature will be colorful guideposts painted on the floor that will direct clients easily from one area of the large building to another. For those sight impaired clients, floor texturing will be employed to accomplish the same goal.

The new employment training center will be used to serve those potential clients who are already on a waiting list, as well as others still to come. There will some shifting of clients between the new center and the two existing ones, so that many clients who currently commute great distances will be able to reduce their transportation time and expenses.

The second building, the arts enrichment center, will be a brand new concept for Southern Nevada's citizens with intellectual disabilities. Opportunity Village managers have visited similar facilities in California and New Mexico to collect information and ideas for the center.

Southern Nevada's municipal recreational and cultural programs and facilities are not designed for people with severe disabilities. Thus, these folks are

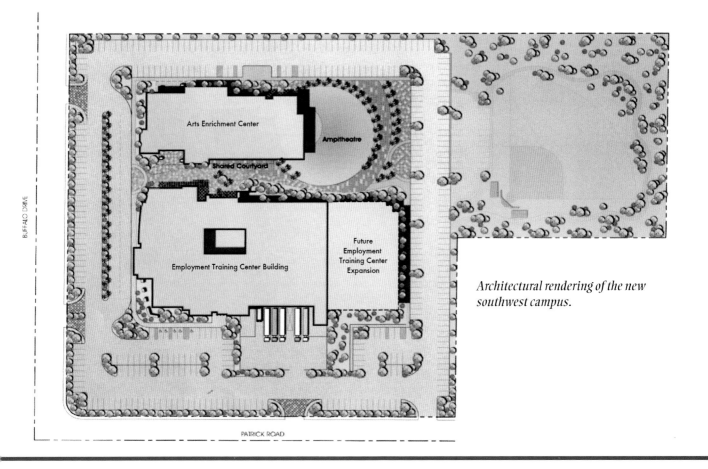

Architectural rendering of the new southwest campus.

left out when it comes to participation in visual art and performing art programs. Once the new facility is open, that will change.

In visual arts, there will be programs in painting, drawing, ceramics, weaving, woodworking, and photography. In the performing arts, people will be able participate in a bell choir, a rhythm band, dance movement, and theater. They will be able to stage dance recitals, band concerts, talent shows and plays. An indoor gymnasium can convert to a theatre, and an outdoor amphitheatre will be available in good weather. There will also be a fitness studio.

A culinary training kitchen will also be in this building, with a commodious serving area for training and actual meal service.

The arts enrichment program already has a financial leg up, thanks to the family of chief development officer Linda Smith. Smith started the "Christopher Smith Endowment for Recreation" years ago to honor her son Chris, a longtime client of Opportunity Village. Today, that endowment fund stands at over $1 million, thanks to generous contributions from Smith herself and many other staff and community members. It is intended that this money will fund some of the arts enrichment programs currently being planned.

The arts enrichment building will be open for use by all people with intellectual disabilities, regardless of where they train or where they are employed. Hours will be expanded so the center can be used after work, and on weekends.

Construction on the new campus starts in the spring of 2007.

As with any project like Opportunity Village's new southwest campus, the first question an organization asks itself is, how can we pay for this? The price tag for the facility and its programs was set at $44 million. Of that figure, nearly $33 million was for the construction itself, while the remaining $11 million was to endow the programs.

Installed as chairman of the fundraising campaign for the new campus was longtime Foundation board member Tom Thomas.

Thomas is a second generation member of Las Vegas' influential Thomas family. His father, banker E. Parry Thomas, is credited with financing the development of hotel/casinos beginning in the mid 1950s, when no other bank would touch them. Much credit for the building of today's Las Vegas is given to the senior Thomas for his pioneering role in financing the city's development.

Tom Thomas attended the University of Utah, receiving an undergraduate degree in finance, and a law degree. In 1986 he returned to Las Vegas as inhouse counsel for Valley Bank of Nevada. He moved through the bank, learning the entire business, until 1992 when it was merged into the giant Bank of America. Realizing he was not cut out for a bureaucratic career in such a large organization, Thomas left

to begin managing an informal real estate partnership that his family and the Mack family had held since 1955. His brother Parry remained in the bank as president of Bank of America Nevada until 1995 when he too joined the real estate partnership, the Thomas & Mack Company, as co-managing partner. Today the company primarily develops commercial real estate and office buildings in Nevada.

Tom Thomas's involvement with Opportunity Village goes back to 1992 when he was asked to serve on the Foundation Board, a position he has held ever since. Thomas is quick to praise both of Opportunity Village's boards of directors, the ARC board that oversees the operations side of the agency, and the Foundation board, which oversees its financial side.

"These are not just boards of important names and companies. These are boards of people who have their hearts committed to what the organization is doing," Thomas said. "These people really roll up their sleeves when it comes time . . . of all the boards I've sat on, I've never seen so much personal buy-in . . . people are not sitting there on assignment; they're there on desire."

Speaking of the southwest campus capital campaign, which has been underway for more than two years, chairman Thomas is quick to share the credit

South elevation of southwest campus.

with his fifty to sixty committee members, who serve on a number of subcommittees. "These people are all leaders in their individual fields," he said. "It's a very diversified group . . . a very talented bunch of people."

The Thomas and the Mack families kicked off the campaign with a generous $3 million contribution.

In a very unusual move for Opportunity Village, which has always remained debt free, the decision was made to begin construction on the southwest campus before the full amount necessary was raised. That will be accomplished by selling tax-free bonds to fund the construction. Thomas pointed out that with construction costs rising at an average of one percent a month, and with the need for the new facility so keen, it's important to begin as quickly as possible. That local banks were willing to undertake the sale of the bonds is testament to Opportunity Village's solid financial reputation, he said.

♥ ♥ ♥

While the new southwest campus may be the most important project on the horizon for Opportunity Village, it is certainly not the only future need being studied. All of the same social and economic uncertainties facing people today — the aging of the population, a diminishing confidence in the Social Security system, unbridled growth in Las Vegas

— are also facing people with intellectual disabilities. But with the latter group, these uncertainties are magnified. For example, an agency like Opportunity Village not only has to worry about the aging of its client population, and how to deal with it, but also about the aging of the clients' caregivers. What happens to a man or woman with an intellectual disability when his only relative and chief caregiver can no longer fulfill that role because of advanced age?

If Opportunity Village doesn't care about this, who does? If Opportunity Village doesn't step in and provide a solution, who will? The answer to those questions is that the government will have to step in, and all taxpayers will be responsible through their taxes.

It is for this reason, and the diminishing supply of group homes in Las Vegas discussed in chapter nine, that the organization is studying the feasibility of getting into the affordable housing business.

"Parents have approached him [Ed Guthrie] . . . about group homes," associate executive director Jean Perry said. Parents prefer to keep their adult child with disabilities at home when possible, because they feel they can provide the best and most loving care for the individual. But they also worry about the time when they will no longer be around to provide that safe nest. These parents also realize that sometimes

North elevation of southwest campus.

group homes, although well meaning, are not able to provide the best care for their loved one.

"They know that Opportunity Village, and the staff at Opportunity Village, care about their son or daughter . . . and they've begged us to open group homes because they know we would give that same level of care," Perry said.

"There is a lack of affordable housing in the Las Vegas area," Ed Guthrie said. "And what most people don't realize is that even affordable housing is not usually affordable for people with severe disabilities."

Guthrie explained that affordable housing is defined as housing for those people who make between sixty percent and eighty percent of the area's medium income. The people served by Opportunity Village, however, earn only thirty percent to forty percent of the median income, or less. "So the normal affordable housing model isn't going to work for our population," Guthrie said.

Thus, Guthrie, emphasized, what the organization is really studying is what kind of housing models will work for their population. However, he is quick to point out that this is not a frontburner issue with Opportunity Village, and that the focus must remain on the growth of core services for the foreseeable future.

The aging of the population also creates another need, a need for expanded senior services for the mentally disabled. This program, which is still in the discussion stage, will become part of the offerings at the new arts and enrichment center.

"We have a lot of individuals who are aging on the employment training center floor," Jean Perry said. "They don't want to give up coming to work because

The aging of the population also creates another need, a need for expanded senior services for the mentally disabled.

it's their social life. But they need a place where they can go and be active, a place that meets more of their needs as they age."

This program would include not only leisure time activities but also activities to help seniors stay fit. It is also a program that Perry plans to have up and running before the completion of the new southwest campus with its arts and enrichment facility.

The failed recreation program discussed in chapter nine will also be restarted under the umbrella of the arts enrichment program.

♥ ♥ ♥

Ed Guthrie is a man who is always looking toward the future. With the opening of the new southwest campus still a year away, he is already thinking about the next expansion.

"Right now we have to look at where the other growth areas of the valley are . . . where will we have to put the fourth campus?" he asked. Indicating the northwest area of the valley, Guthrie added, "One of our guiding visions is that . . . no matter where you live in the Las Vegas metro area, we want you to be able to get to our services within a forty-five minute bus ride."

♥ ♥ ♥

It's impossible to look at the future and not say at least a few words about a growing problem for all non-profits and not-for-profits: the diminishing supply of college graduates entering public service careers.

In April 2006 the Public Interest Research Group issued a report entitled "Paying Back, Not Giving Back," that discusses growing student debt and its impact on public service jobs. In the past decade, the report states, government support for higher education has declined, forcing tuition and fees much higher. As a result, two-thirds of all four year college graduates in 2004 left school with student debt, double the figure from a decade earlier. This has resulted in many graduating students bypassing public service careers for more lucrative private sector jobs.

"The prospect of burdensome debt likely deters skilled and dedicated college graduates from entering and staying in important careers . . . [like] helping the country's most vulnerable populations," the report states.

The report also cites a state by state ranking of the percentage of public university four-year students who graduate with debt exceeding what is described as "manageable levels." The rankings represent those who would opt for teaching jobs in the named state, not nonprofit jobs; but the figures are good indicators. For Nevada, the figure is thirty-four percent, placing it seventeenth among the fifty states. The U. S. Average is 23.2 percent.

While these figures certainly do not signal a death knell for organizations like Opportunity Village as they attempt to recruit bright young people, they do raise a warning flag. "This certainly can impact us in the future," responded Human Resources Director Kathy Ferguson. However, she pointed out, Opportunity Village ameliorates the problem to some degree by the educational support it provides for employees who have not yet earned a degree.

♥ ♥ ♥

Afterword

Helping Hands, Helping Hearts: The Story of Opportunity Village is the fourth book I have written since retiring five years ago. The first two were historical biographies, and I had become quite comfortable working in that genre. Set me down in the special collections department of a large library, or in the dank basement of a New England town clerk's office searching through musty, 300-year-old town records, and I am one happy fellow. But as I approached this Opportunity Village project, I was a little nervous.

I knew the first part of the book would be similar to the work I had done before, so I was in my comfort zone. But what of the second part, where I had to dissect the organization to see what makes it so unique? How would I approach that part; how would I tell that story?

In the end, of course, I decided to let those who live the story every day tell it in their own words. The honesty and the eloquence of Opportunity Village's clients, their parents, the wonderful staff, the volunteers, and the supportive community made my job an easy one. I had only to connect the dots and the story told itself.

I found the project an amazing and rewarding experience. I also made a lot of new friends, a priceless recompense for my efforts. As I now prepare to return to my libraries and dank basements for my next historical biography, I take with me a warm glow from having authored this book.

I sincerely hope you have enjoyed reading it as much as I enjoyed writing it.

— Jack Harpster

Take A Tour

Opportunity Village invites you — and I strongly encourage you — to arrange a tour of their facilities. Call 702-259-3741 or visit www.opportunityvillage.org. You won't regret a moment of the time spent.

BIBLIOGRAPHY

American Association on Mental Retardation, Washington D. C. www.AAMR.org.

Angrosino, Michael V. *Opportunity House: Ethnographic Stories of Mental Retardation.* Walnut Creek CA: AtlaMira, 1998.

ARC, Silver Spring, Maryland. www.thearc.org.

Barbeito, Carol L., and Jack P. Bowman. *Nonprofit Compensation and Benefits Practices.* New York: Applied Research and Development Institute Intl., 1998.

Carver, John N., and Nellie Enders Carver. *The Family of the Retarded Child.* Syracuse: Syracuse University Division of Special Education and Rehabilitation, 1972.

Dondero, Harvey N. *History of Clark County Schools.* Privately Published, 1986.

Dougan, Terrell, Lyn Isbell and Patricia Vyas, eds. *We Have Been There: Families Share The Joys and Struggles of Living with Mental Retardation.* Nashville: Abingdon, 1983.

Gray, Raymond Guild. *The Organization of a County School District; A Case Study of A Process of District Consolidation and Administrative Reorganization.* Ph.D. Diss., Stanford University, 1958.

Hopkins, A. D., and K. J. Kent, eds. *The First 100: Portraits of the Men and Women Who Shaped Las Vegas.* Las Vegas; Huntington, 1999.

Jones, Florence. "Tribute to Dessie Bailey." Speech given at Service League Sustaining Members Party, May 23, 1963. Opportunity Village History Files, Las Vegas Nevada.

Kingsley, Jason, and Mitchell Levitz. *Count on Us: Growing up with Down Syndrome.* New York: Harcourt Brace, 1994.

The Kitsap Sun, Bremerton, Washington.

Las Vegas Perspective, 2005. Las Vegas, Nevada.

Las Vegas Review–Journal, Las Vegas, Nevada.

Las Vegas Sun, Las Vegas, Nevada.

Macklin, Ruth, and Willard Gaylin, eds. *Mental Retardation and Sterilization: A Problem of Competency and Paternalism.* New York: Plenum, 1981.

Moehring, Eugene P., and Michael S. Green. *Las Vegas: A Centennial History.* Reno: University of Nevada Press, 2005.

Noll, Steven, and James W. Trent, eds. *Mental Retardation in America: a Historical Reader.* New York: New York University Press, 2004.

Opportunity Village, Our Fiftieth Anniversary. Las Vegas: Opportunity Village, 2004.

Opportunity Village. www.opportunityvillage.org.

Paher, Stanley W. *Las Vegas: As It Began – As It Grew.* Las Vegas: Nevada Publications, 1971.

Public Interest Research Group. "Paying Back, Not Giving Back." State PIRG's Higher Education Project. www.uspirg.org/home/reports/report-archives/

Reno Gazette Journal, Reno, Nevada.

Rogers, Dale Evans. *Angel Unaware.* Westwood, New Jersey: Fleming H. Revell, 1953.

Sarason, Seymore B., and John Doris. *Educational Handicap, Public Policy and Social History: A Broadened Perspective on Mental Retardation.* New York: Free Press, 1979.

Smithsonian Magazine. "Medical Sleuth," by Tom Shachtman. February, 2006.

Squires, Charles P., and Delphine Squires. *Las Vegas, Nevada: It's Romance and History.* Unpublished manuscript, 1955. Special Collections Department, University of Nevada Las Vegas Library.

Trent, James W. *Inventing the Feeble Mind: A History of Mental Retardation in the United States.* Berkeley: University of California Press, 1994.

Valley Times, Las Vegas, Nevada.

Variety Clubs, International. www.varietychildrenscharity.org.

Variety Club, Pittsburgh, Pennsylvania. www.varietytent1.org.

Variety Clubs. U. S. www.usvariety.org

Variety School for Special Education, "Handbook of Information, 1952–1953." In the historical files of Opportunity Village, Las Vegas, Nevada.

White, Harry A., as told to B. J. Lawry. *Riding Bareback to Las Vegas.* New York: Vantage Press, 1985.

Whitely, Joan Burkhart. *Young Las Vegas, 1905–1931: Before the Future Found Us.* Las Vegas: Stephens Press, 2005.

Wright, Frank. *Nevada Yesterdays: Short Looks at Las Vegas History.* Las Vegas: Stephens Press, 2005.

Photo Credits

Jacket (front): Richard Bailey

Book cover: Courtesy of Opportunity Village

Page 12: Courtesy of Nevada State Museum and Historical Society, Las Vegas

Page 15: Courtesy of Davis Collection, University of Nevada, Las Vegas Library

Page 17, 19, 20: Courtesy of Opportunity Village

Page 28: Courtesy of Nevada State Museum and Historical Society, Las Vegas

Page 31: Courtesy of Opportunity Village

Page 33, 34: Courtesy of Variety, The Children's Charity

Page 35: Courtesy of Joylin Vandenberg

Page 36: Courtesy of Variety, The Children's Charity

Page 38, 41: Courtesy of Opportunity Village

Page 42: Top: Courtesy of Nevada State Museum and Historical Archives, Las Vegas; Center and bottom: Courtesy of University of Nevada, Las Vegas, Special Collections

Page 43: Courtesy of Elbert Edwards Collection, University of Nevada, Las Vegas Library

Page 44: Courtesy of Southern Nevada Educators Collection, University of Nevada, Las Vegas Library

Page 45: Both, Courtesy of Opportunity Village

Page 48, 51: Courtesy of Opportunity Village

Page 52: Both, Courtesy of Joylin Vandenberg

Page 53: Both, Courtesy of Opportunity Village

Page 54: Courtesy of Joylin Vandeberg

Page 56, 57: Courtesy of Opportunity Village

Page 58: Courtesy of *The Las Vegas Review-Journal*

Page 61, 64, 66, 70, 75, 77: Courtesy of Opportunity Village

Page 78: , 80, 84, 87–93, 96, 97, 99, 101–102, 109: Courtesy of Opportunity Village

Page 115: All, Courtesy of Opportunity Village

Page 117: All, Courtesy of Opportunity Village

Page 122, 125–126, 135: Courtesy of Opportunity Village

Page 137: Courtesy of Fledia Sardelli

Page 140–141: All, Courtesy of Opportunity Village

Page 143–146: All, Courtesy of Variety, The Children's Charity

Page 149–150: All, Courtesy of Variety, The Children's Charity

Page 152–154: All, Courtesy of Opportunity Village

Page 155: Top, Courtesy of Mike Smith; Bottom: Courtesy of Opportunity Village

Page 156–158: All, Courtesy of Opportunity Village

Page 159: Courtesy of *The Las Vegas Review-Journal*

Page 160–166: All, Courtesy of Opportunity Village

Page 168: Courtesy of Opportunity Village

Page 175–177: Courtesy of Opportunity Village